KORN/FERRY INTERNATIONAL

powered by LOMINGER ⚙

FYI
For Learning Agility™

Robert W. Eichinger, Michael M. Lombardo,
& Cara C. Capretta

FYI For Learning Agility™

(Formerly known as FYI for Talent Management™)

Tel. +1 952-345-3610
Tel. +1 877-345-3610 (US/Canada)
Fax. +1 952-345-3601
www.kornferry.com
www.lominger.com

ISBN 978-1-933578-21-7

Item number 82040

FYI for Learning Agility™ 1st Edition Printings:

	version 04.1a 1st—05/04
	version 04.1b 2nd—10/04
FYI for Talent Management™	version 06.1a 3rd—06/06
	version 07.1a 4th—07/07
FYI for Learning Agility™	version 10.1a 1st—01/10

Table of Contents

Introduction Intro-1
About the Authors Intro-9
Fundamentals of Learning Agility Intro-11

Factor I – Mental Agility 1
Dimension 1. Broad Scanner 3
Dimension 2. Complexity 9
Dimension 3. Connector 15
Dimension 4. Critical Thinker 21
Dimension 5. Easy Shifter 27
Dimension 6. Essence 33
Dimension 7. Inquisitive 39
Dimension 8. Solution Finder 45

Factor II – People Agility 51
Dimension 9. Agile Communicator 53
Dimension 10. Conflict Manager 59
Dimension 11. Cool Transactor 65
Dimension 12. Helps Others Succeed 71
Dimension 13. Light Touch 77
Dimension 14. Open Minded 83
Dimension 15. People Smart 89
Dimension 16. Personal Learner 95
Dimension 17. Responds to Feedback 101
Dimension 18. Role Flexibility 107
Dimension 19. Self-Aware 113

Factor III – Change Agility 119
Dimension 20. Experimenter 121
Dimension 21. Innovation Manager 127
Dimension 22. Taking the Heat 135
Dimension 23. Visioning 143

Factor IV – Results Agility 151
Dimension 24. Inspires Others 153
Dimension 25. Delivers Results 161
Dimension 26. Drive 167
Dimension 27. Presence 173

Appendix A
Creating a Development Plan A-1

Appendix B
Competency Summary B-1

Introduction

To be good at anything requires some knowledge, skills, and technical know-how. What separates the remarkable from the good is the ability to adjust, adapt, respond, and be resourceful in the face of change. People with this ability perform well under first-time, challenging conditions. These are people we call **learning agile**.* The learning agile take meaning from the past and fit it into a different challenge they are facing. They are able to answer the question: "What do you do when you don't know what to do?" When it comes to talent and potential, learning agility separates the best from the rest. In this book, we present tips and strategies to help people reach the highest levels in learning agility.

Learning agility is measured using the Choices Architect® 2nd Edition, a validated 81-Item assessment organized into 4 Factors and 27 Dimensions. This book addresses the development of learning agility at the Dimension level.

For more information on the foundations of learning agility, refer to the Fundamentals of Learning Agility chapter in this book.

Who is this book for?

This book was designed for any motivated person seeking to develop skills that lead to increased learning agility. The suggestions provided are aimed at gaining insight on learning strengths and remedying skill needs. The content will also help anyone who is serving as a manager, mentor, or feedback giver.

We know that anyone who has not yet recognized and accepted a learning agility need, limitation, weakness, or development opportunity will not be helped by what's in this book. If you are in denial, rationalizing, confused, or being defensive about having needs, nothing in this book will help.

People who do accept that they have a need to increase their learning agility but do not have the motivation, drive, urgency, or energy to do anything about it also won't be helped by what's in this book.

So, this book is intended for people who believe they have a need and want to do something about it. There are hundreds of tips and workarounds in this book that will help you develop skills that lead to increased learning agility.

The structure of this book:

Each of the 27 chapters addresses one of the Dimensions of learning agility and includes the following sections:

1. **Definition** – What skilled and unskilled look like for this Dimension of learning agility. As all Dimensions lie in one of four Choices Architect® 2nd Edition Factors, we include a High and Low definition of the Factor as well so you can put the Dimension into context. The High and Low Factor definitions precede the first Dimension in each Factor.

2. **Items** – The specific Items in Choices Architect® 2nd Edition used to measure this Dimension.

3. **Leadership Architect® Competencies Most Associated with This Dimension** – This indicates which of the 67 Competencies in the Leadership Architect® Library are either strongly, moderately, or lightly related to this Dimension. Using the competency lists, you can compare a person who has had 360° feedback on competencies against the Dimension. Also, the lists can serve as a guide as you study additional remedies from the *FYI For Your Improvement™* book.

4. **Some Causes** – We list numerous reasons why you might have this need. Use these to specify what your need looks like exactly. What causes a need might be very different for each individual. The difference might lead to quite different remedies. You might not listen because you are very impatient with everything and everyone. You just don't take the time to listen. On the other hand, you might not listen because you don't think anyone else is smarter than you are. Or you might not listen because you avoid feedback and are very defensive. Even though the weakness is the same—you don't listen—the underlying cause is quite different and the fix or remedy will be completely different.

5. **Developmental Difficulty** – Each Dimension is classified as Easier, Moderate, or Harder to develop. This will help you set your expectations regarding the scope and speed of your development.

6. **The Map** – A description of the Dimension to provide a broad context. The map explains key elements of the Dimension and their importance.

7. **Some Remedies** – Suggestions for actions that you can take to increase effectiveness in each Dimension. Based on our research and experience, these are the tips that are most likely to work. Choose a few to include in your development plan. Although a few may be longer-term, most are things you can start working on today. For each Dimension, we include one or more workarounds, if you decide to take an indirect route to working on the need.

8. **More Help?** We have included 10 tips from *FYI For Your Improvement*™ for each of the items measuring this Dimension.

9. **Jobs That Would Add Skills in This Dimension** – Most development of learning agility takes place when it has to, under challenging job conditions. Lots of people pause at this section. Why suggest a job here? I already have a job or I don't want to do this one or it would be risky for me to get in such a job (e.g., a strategic planning job when I'm lousy at making connections). If this is your last job or you have no career ambition to do anything different or at a higher level, skip this section. Otherwise read on.

   THIS SECTION IS HERE BECAUSE:
   - The number one developer of competence by far is stretching, challenging jobs—not feedback, not courses, not role models, but jobs where you develop and exercise significant and varied competencies. If you really want to grow, these are the best places to do it.
   - If you are ambitious, these are the jobs that matter most for long-term success. In the Center for Creative Leadership studies, executives who remained successful had been tested in many of the jobs you'll see in this section.
   - You have a rich opportunity to use your job to learn better from experience. What specifically about the job demands that you work on this need? Write down these challenges; focus your development on them.

10. **Part-Time Assignments That Would Add Skills in This Dimension** – Unless you have challenging job tasks where you must perform and have a real risk of failing, not much development will occur. This is the essence of action learning or learning from experience—not practice, not trying things out, but getting better in order to perform and succeed. Take the example of listening skills, a common need. Everyone has had a million chances (practices) to listen better but they don't, usually because there are some people or some situations they've chosen to avoid. They have passed up the opportunity for practice and have gotten away with it. To learn to listen better, they would do well to participate in a tough negotiation or run a task force of experts in an area in which they lack expertise. Get the idea? It's listen or else you can't do the job. It's listen or fail. Any plan you write must have "perform this or else" tasks in it to work. Otherwise, you'll revert to your old ways. To use these tasks, shape them to your job and organization. What tasks like these are available? If you have a significant need (you are really weak in this area), start with smaller challenges and build up to the tougher ones.

11. **Suggested Readings** – We have added hundreds of books to help you go beyond the tips we present in these pages. Each of the 27 chapters in *FYI for Learning Agility*™ has 10 to 20 sources for further reading.

WE USED THESE SELECTION CRITERIA:
- ROI – Is there a significant and immediate payoff for reading this book? Are there suggestions busy people can implement?
- Organization – Is the book well-laid-out? Is it easy to find what you are looking for?
- Ease – Is it well-written?
- Solid – Is the advice more than opinion?
- Prolific – Are there lots of tips and examples?
- Available – Is the book available?

What are the most effective ways to increase learning agility?

You can do two things. You can improve or use workarounds:

IMPROVEMENT STRATEGIES
You can work to improve. You can work on your weak areas that are mission critical to what you do. We recommend a six-pronged strategy:

1. **Find and use your learning strengths.** Find your highest Factor or cluster of Dimensions (there are 27 learning themes) and leverage them. If you excel at seeing problems differently, get into more situations that allow you to hone your strengths.

2. **Neutralize your weaker learning areas.** If you're not terribly personable or hate to deal with conflict, your first goal should be to turn this from a negative to a neutral. Start small, using the tips in this guide.

3. **Seek further feedback.** Little happens without feedback tied to a goal. Get a developmental partner, get feedback a year from now on Choices Architect® 2nd Edition, ask for an Interview Architect® Learning From Experience™ (LFE) interview, poll people you work with about what you should keep doing, keep doing with slight modifications, stop doing, and start doing.

4. **Test the unknown.** Many learning dimensions you might be low on reflect lack of experience that we call an untested area. Maybe you don't deal with change well, but have never led a change effort. Pick something small that needs doing, and give it a try using the tips from the Dimensions in Factor III – Change Agility.

5. **Go against your natural grain.** We call these GAG (Going Against your natural Grain). GAG because it is uncomfortable. If you're ambitious or if you seek a different kind of job, you'll have to work on your downsides

more vigorously than the suggestion in number 2 above. Few succeed in a different job by simply repeating past successful behavior. This is a strong lesson from career research. You'll have to stretch in uncomfortable areas. For example, whether you gravitate toward team building or not, you can learn the behaviors of excellent team builders. You might even come to enjoy it. It's important not to confuse what you like to do with what's necessary to do.

6. **You don't have to be good at everything.** Most successful leaders have four to six major strengths but tend to lack glaring weaknesses. Developing in all 27 Dimensions of Choices Architect® is unlikely. Use the strategies above to select wisely.

If directly working on improvement is not useful at the moment, use the indirect strategy of workarounds:

WORKAROUND STRATEGIES

Work around the weakness. This involves using other resources to get the same thing done. While there may or may not be any learning attached to the workaround, this accomplishes what has to be done without directly addressing the personal need. Essential to this approach is self-knowledge. You have to know you have the need and acknowledge its importance. Some general workaround tips follow.

General Workaround Tips

The goal of a workaround is to reduce the noise caused by having the need. What follows is a general workaround list of tips that would apply to many different weaknesses or needs:

- People workarounds...
  Find an internal or external person to stand in for you when the weakness is in play. This could be a peer, a friend, someone from your staff, or a consultant. For example, if you are a marginal presenter, get someone who is a good presenter to present your material. Hire people for your team who are good in the areas you are not. Delegate the tasks that bring the weakness into play.

- Task workarounds...
  Trade tasks or share tasks with a peer. For example, you help a peer with his or her strategic planning, and he or she helps you with your presentations to senior management. Structure the weakness out. Redesign your job (with your boss) so that you are not responsible for the task(s) that brings your weakness into play. Change your job so that you no longer have to give lots of speeches to strangers. Assign that task to another unit.

- ■ **Change workarounds...**
  If you decide that you don't want to work on your needs, do an honest assessment of your strengths and find an organization, a job, another unit, or another career that fits those strengths. If you are in sales promotion and are not a comfortable presenter or cold caller, then find a sales job where leads are provided or customers come to you, or consider marketing analysis where those two requirements are greatly decreased.

- ■ **Self workarounds...**
  Acknowledge your weaknesses and be honest with yourself and others. Research shows that admitting weaknesses (within limits) actually increases people's evaluations of you. So if you start by saying, "As most of you know, speaking is not one of my strengths," people will not be as critical. Make a conscious decision to live with a weakness. If you decide not to address the need, concentrate harder on the things you do well.

How do I use this book?

1. **Determine the need.** From regular feedback or use of the Choices Architect® Sort Cards or eChoices™ Online Survey, try to determine what the need is and which needs to work on. Sometimes even excellent feedback can identify the wrong need. Even if everyone agrees that you have problems managing conflict (Dimension 10), the question is why? Maybe the real problem is due to your not being open to others' opinions (Dimension 14) or not being able to read people's reactions (Dimension 15). So, if none or only a few of the tips for your identified need seem to make sense, check other likely Dimensions to see if the need is more likely one of these.

2. **Read the unskilled and skilled definitions for the need.** Which bullet points describe the need best? Look to the skilled definition. How do you want to act when you are done working on this need? This is the before and after picture.

3. **Look at the Leadership Architect® Competencies most associated with the need.** Each competency has a complete development plan associated with it in *FYI For Your Improvement*™ or the *Career Architect® Development Planner*. It may be that you will need to build or modify your personal development plan(s) to increase your learning agility.

4. **Check the causes that might apply.** Many developmental efforts have floundered because the plan attacked the wrong problem. Causes get to "why" you may have a need in this Dimension. Write down your specific need—what it looks like, what causes it, whom it plays out with, and in what situations.

5. Take note of the Developmental Difficulty level of the Dimension. Some weaknesses are tougher to fix than others. Knowing the relative difficulty of working on a need will help set you up for success.

6. Read the map for the Dimension. The map gives the lay of the land. It reviews the general case of the behavior, how it operates, and why it's important. The map sets context and helps clarify what the Dimension is all about.

7. Look at the remedies and pick the specific ones that apply. Each topic is written against a specific manifestation of being unskilled at the Dimension. It is unlikely that all of the topics or remedies will apply to any person. Pick a few that apply. Start small. Think back to the causes you checked and the "why it's important" noted from the map.

8. Look at the suggested readings listed. They might also be helpful to deepen your understanding on your needs and to help put together the action plan.

9. Look at the general plan. Appendix A lists 10 ways to develop in any area. Pick any of those that seem to fit. This general, or universal, plan can be used as a basic core for any plan.

10. Lay out a plan and a schedule. The plan should include at least three items you will work on immediately. Use the development plan in Appendix A. Measure the number of times you do this or don't do that and record these efforts so you can track improvement. Set a specific time frame of no more than a month to try these items repeatedly. If the time frame is longer or indefinite, you will be less likely to do anything. Start today.

FYI for Learning Agility™ contains numerous resources:

- Tips for the 27 learning agility Dimensions are listed in each corresponding chapter of this book.
- Appendix A contains a general, or universal, plan for attacking any developmental need—anything you want to get better at doing—along with sample templates to use when creating a plan.
- Appendix B contains the Competency Summary: A listing of the 22 Leadership Architect® Competencies that are most associated with the 27 Choices Architect® 2nd Edition Dimensions.

Additional references:

This book can be used as a stand-alone assessment and development resource in conjunction with the Choices Architect® 2nd Edition Sort Cards or eChoices™ Online Survey, or in conjunction with *FYI For Your Improvement*™—a comprehensive book for individual development that includes a full library of leadership competencies and tips. *FYI For Your Improvement*™ contains 10 tips for each of the 67 Leadership Architect® Competencies and the 19 Career Stallers and Stoppers identified in research over the decades. More extensive developmental recommendations on the same material are contained in the *Career Architect® Development Planner*. A subset of the 67 Leadership Architect® Competencies most closely linked to a particular Dimension appears toward the beginning of each chapter.

About the Authors

Robert W. Eichinger

Bob Eichinger is Vice Chairman of the Korn/Ferry Institute for Korn/Ferry International. Prior to Korn/Ferry's acquisition of Lominger International, he was cofounder and CEO of Lominger Limited, Inc. and cocreator of the Leadership Architect® Suite of management, executive, and organizational development tools. During his 40+ year career, he has worked inside companies such as PepsiCo and Pillsbury, and as a consultant in Fortune 500 companies in the United States, Europe, Japan, Canada, and Australia. Dr. Eichinger lectures extensively on the topic of executive and management development and has served on the Board of the Human Resource Planning Society. He has worked as a coach with more than 1,000 managers and executives. Some of his books include *The Leadership Machine*, written with Mike Lombardo, *100 Things You Need to Know: Best People Practices for Managers & HR*, written with Mike Lombardo and Dave Ulrich, and *FYI for Strategic Effectiveness*™, written with Kim Ruyle and Dave Ulrich.

Michael M. Lombardo

Mike Lombardo has over 30 years experience in executive and management research and in executive coaching. He is one of the founders of Lominger Limited, Inc., publishers of the Leadership Architect® Suite. With Bob Eichinger, Mike has authored 40 products for the suite, including *The Leadership Machine*, *FYI For Your Improvement*™, the *Career Architect*®, *Choices Architect*®, and VOICES®. During his 15 years at the Center for Creative Leadership, Mike was a coauthor of *The Lessons of Experience*, which detailed which learnings from experience can teach the competencies needed to be successful. He also coauthored the research on executive derailment revealing how personal flaws and overdone strengths caused otherwise effective executives to get into career trouble, Benchmarks®, a 360° feedback instrument, and the Looking Glass® simulation. Mike has won four national awards for research on managerial and executive development.

Cara C. Capretta

Cara Capretta is a former Senior Partner of Korn/Ferry Leadership and Talent Consulting. Prior to Korn/Ferry's acquisition of Lominger International in 2006, she was President and Chief Operating Officer at Lominger. She is the coauthor of *FYI for Talent Management*™, a book for developing learning agility—a concept that is strongly connected to being a "high potential," and coauthor of *The Interview Architect*®, a book for developing competency-based interview guides. Cara has over 15 years of practical experience working with leaders, teams, and organizations on development. Prior to joining Lominger, she was the Director of Executive Development for Nationwide, a Fortune 500 insurance company, where she designed and implemented a succession planning system to identify, develop, and place global talent in an organization with over 30,000 employees. She currently resides in Columbus, Ohio.

Fundamentals of Learning Agility

When the winds of change rage, some build shelters while others build windmills.
– A Chinese proverb

"So what makes you think Viktor is a high potential?"

"Well, he is an outstanding performer. He blew away the top line numbers last year and was still able to keep costs down. He's the expert we rely on. He always does what I ask him to do. He gets along with everyone at the company. He's a great mentor. He'd be tough to replace, that's for sure!"

And...

"Viktor consistently volunteers to work overtime and comes in on weekends if I need him. He always has a smile on his face. In fact, one time last year when I was in the hospital with an appendicitis attack and missed a week of work, Viktor managed the department seamlessly. I can depend on him."

Such conversations occur every year during talent review meetings in organizations around the world. Managers strongly perceive some of their employees to be high potentials and seek to groom them for senior-level executive positions. In their eyes, these employees have "the right stuff." But do they really? Are we sure? How do we know? And if they really are high potentials, how should we develop them so they can be ready for future promotions?

The development of a company's future leaders is widely recognized as a top business priority in most organizations today (Blanchard, 2007; Dychtwald, Erickson, & Morison, 2006). Unfortunately, many companies appear to do a poor job at identifying which employees truly are high potentials. According to several recent studies, only about one-half of companies report having a high potential identification program (Howard, 2009; Jerusalim & Hausdorf, 2007; Wells, 2003). And those companies that do have programs frequently select individuals based on factors not necessarily related to potential, such as personal experience with the person, performance review ratings, and past performance results (Jerusalim & Hausdorf, 2007). Even when companies do select the right employees, their subsequent development often is unsystematic and ineffective.

Many corporate executives candidly admit that they are dissatisfied with their company's initiatives for developing leaders (Charan, 2005). The issue is *not* that companies don't develop people. Development happens in all companies. Rather, the real issue is that development is not planful or systematic. Many companies don't understand how development happens. They don't know when to develop which competencies in what situations. Worse yet, they identify the wrong people for development. That is not to say that companies shouldn't view all of their employees as important. Obviously, they are. However, some employees have much more potential for future leadership positions than others. In particular, organizations should focus their leadership development efforts on those high potentials.

The proper assessment, identification, and development of high potentials represents one of the key components of best-in-class leadership development programs (Hewitt Associates, 2005). In this chapter, we review what makes an employee a high potential, or so-called "hipo." We make an important distinction between a high potential, a high professional, and a high performer. We introduce the term, *learning agility,* as a key indicator of leadership potential and articulate its historical background. Subsequently, we review learning agility within the broader context of leadership. The eChoices™ Online Survey is presented as a psychometrically validated assessment of the concept, and relevant empirical findings are highlighted. Finally, we discuss how learning agility can be used to develop the next generation of leaders in the workforce.

Distinguishing Between High Potentials, High Professionals, and High Performers

High potentials are special people. Sure, they perform their jobs exceedingly well. They are competent. They are dependable and reliable. They are motivated. They willingly volunteer to be on nearly any task force or assignment that must be done. They go the extra mile. However, more importantly, they are agile learners—they like experimenting, trying new things. They are highly curious. Research suggests the following characteristics are common among high potential employees:

- Easily learn new tasks and functions.
- Enjoy and deal well with ambiguity and complexity.
- Don't accept the status quo.
- Are impatient.
- Like to try new things, different approaches.
- Tend to push the envelope.
- When things fail, they are willing to take the heat.

Such employees are excellent candidates for senior general management and leadership positions.

In contrast, *high professionals* are technical experts in a defined area or function. They have a proven track record of superior performance year after year. Some common features of high professionals include:

- Are passionate about what they do.
- Love their role in the organization and the contributions they make.
- Likely possess a depth of organizational knowledge.
- Are viewed as trusted resources within the organization.
- Are widely recognized outside the company for their knowledge and expertise.
- Tend to be excellent at mentoring and developing people.
- Frequently, do not aspire to broader management roles.

Both high potentials and high professionals are critical to an organization's future success. Both can be difficult to replace. Obviously, both are needed. However, their organizational contributions—current and future—are quite different.

In addition, we need to understand that there is a clear difference between *high performers* and high potentials. Not all high performers are high potentials. Research suggests that only about 30% of high performers can be classified as high potentials (Corporate Leadership Council, 2005). Also worth noting is that not all high potentials are high performers, but the percentage is much, much higher. The same study found that about 93% of high potentials perform at a high level.

Learning Agility: A Primary Indicator of High Potential

In 2000, Michael Lombardo and Robert Eichinger published an article entitled "High Potentials As High Learners." It highlighted the concept of learning agility and presented their findings on the relationship between learning agility and leadership potential. The authors theorized that potential cannot be fully detected from what an individual already demonstrates on the job. Rather, it requires that the individual do something new or different. In the view of Lombardo and Eichinger, potential involves learning new skills to perform in new, very often, first-time situations. They speculated that people differ in their aptitude to learn from their experiences. It is this capability to learn from experience which differentiates high potentials from others (McCall, Lombardo, & Morrison, 1988).

The implication is that organizations should assess individuals' learning agility to identify truly high potentials for future leadership positions. This approach differed from most traditional practices at that time. Previously, most companies developed and promoted their high performers without realizing that current performance in one situation does not guarantee high performance in a different one. As mentioned, it has been observed that less than 30% of an organization's high performers have the *potential* to rise to and succeed in broader senior-level, critical positions. Consequently, organizations would be wise to strengthen their high potential assessment by adding learning agility to an individual's success profile. According to Lombardo and Eichinger, organizations need to measure "the willingness and ability to learn new competencies in order to perform under first-time, tough, or different conditions" (Lombardo & Eichinger, 2000, p. 323).

Many different researchers have contributed to the evolution of learning agility as an important predictor of high potential identification. The longitudinal studies conducted at AT&T observed that people who had been assessed low for potential were frequently more successful than expected if they had developmental opportunities (see Howard & Bray, 1988; Bray, Campbell, & Grant, 1974). Sternberg and his colleagues emphasized "practical intelligence" as a critical part of overall intelligence (Sternberg, 1985, 1997; Sternberg, Wagner, Williams, & Horvath, 1995). Such characteristics as being street smart, interpersonal savvy, and possessing common sense were important in "practical intelligence" or "learning intelligence." These authors found that learning intelligence (i.e., learning agility) was much more predictive of individual success than basic IQ.

Research and application of learning agility is not limited to certain industries or types of organizations. For example, the United States military has shown a particular interest in identifying and developing learning-agile leaders. The military's mission in both conflict and peacekeeping activities has evolved considerably in recent years. Today, military personnel are required to play multiple roles, often during the course of a single day. Adaptability and quick learning are essential to navigate the situations soldiers face on a continuous basis. The difference in these cases, literally, could be life or death. Many of the findings from the military's research can be applied to the development of learning agility in other settings. Wong (2004) focused on the environmental drivers that promote the development of adaptive behaviors and identified the key elements of complexity, unpredictability, and ambiguity. Officers who responded constructively to these elements demonstrated higher levels of independence, initiative, innovation, and confidence. Gehler (2005) concluded that agile leaders need to be supported by agile institutions. Specifically, Gehler suggested that training efforts need to be accelerated, dynamic, and experience-based to support the development of agile capabilities. Mueller-Hanson, White, Dorsey, and Pulakos (2005) recommended early and frequent exposure to training experiences that call for adaptive responses.

They indicated soldiers should have numerous and diverse opportunities to apply the lessons learned, receive feedback, and then apply again.

In general, the formulation of the concept of learning agility is rooted largely in two streams of research. Both groups of research studies were conducted at the Center for Creative Leadership (CCL). One series of studies is referred to as "The Lessons of Experience," and examined what leadership competencies were most important for success in organizational promotions. The other series of studies investigated reasons why executives derail. We review both research streams in the next section of the chapter.

THE LESSONS OF EXPERIENCE

By the early 1980s, researchers gradually recognized that it was not possible to provide a comprehensive summary of predisposing characteristics of effective leadership. Leadership seemed to be a product of growing up and gaining managerial experience. However, researchers continued to have a limited knowledge of how experience actually develops managers. Not all experiences appeared to be created equally. The question remained: "What experiences have the most developmental impact?" And, "Who will benefit most from such experiences?" Without understanding how people learn and grow from their experiences, organizations cannot fully take advantage of work-related assignments and job tasks as developmental opportunities.

The Center for Creative Leadership conducted a series of studies to understand how executives learn from their work experiences. Corporate executives were interviewed and asked to describe key events in their careers that caused the most learning. Specifically, the following two questions were probed: (1) What specifically happened on the job, and (2) What did they learn from the event. Researchers interviewed 191 executives from six major corporations. Descriptions of the 616 events and 1,547 corresponding lessons were tabulated. The analyses and results are summarized in the book aptly titled *The Lessons of Experience* (McCall et al., 1988). Two findings had a lasting impact on the practice of leadership development. First, the rule of 70:20:10 was coined. It was discovered that approximately 70% of leadership development occurs primarily from job assignments, 20% from people, and only a small portion (roughly 10%) from traditional classroom education. Subsequently, this rule has been supported by other studies (see McCall & Hollenbeck, 2002).

The second important finding—one that is the most relevant here—is that people significantly differ as learners from experience. Some individuals learn more quickly and learn more content than others. Learning and development requires that individuals move away from their comfort zone, their habits, and their routines. The researchers observed that the most developmental experiences are challenging, stretching, and difficult. The best learning experiences are emotional, require us to take risks, and tend to have real-life consequences (Lombardo & Eichinger, 2004). The journey tends to be unpleasant. Learners have to be resilient and non-defensive. Individuals have to possess a strong need for growth. Overall, this research reveals that the willingness and ability to learn from experience separates high potentials from others. The importance of learning from experience for successful executives has been echoed by many other leadership researchers (e.g., Bennis & Thomas, 2002).

EXECUTIVE DERAILMENT

A second stream of research that framed the development of learning agility was conducted at CCL nearly two decades ago (Lombardo & Eichinger, 1989; Lombardo, Ruderman, & McCauley, 1988; McCall & Lombardo, 1983; Morrison, White, & Van Velsor, 1987 [Updated ed. 1994]; Van Velsor & Leslie, 1995). These studies compared successful versus derailed executives. Derailed executives were defined as those individuals who were identified as high potentials, promoted, often promoted again, only to ultimately fail. This research produced consistent findings across time, hierarchical levels, national culture, gender, and organizations.

Overall, the authors found that *both* successful and derailed executives were (a) very bright, (b) had been identified as high potentials *early* in their careers, (c) possessed outstanding records of achievement, and (d) were ambitious and willing to sacrifice. Both groups of executives also possessed very few personal flaws. However, one derailment factor was observed repeatedly. The authors found that derailed executives were unable or unwilling to change or adapt. They relied too much on a narrow set of work skills. The derailed leaders generally had a series of prior successes, but typically in very similar organizational situations. On the other hand, successful executives usually had a diverse set of experiences in a variety of settings. For most of the leaders who had derailed, their comparative technical superiority was a source of success at lower levels of leadership. However, when they ascended to the higher levels, this strength became a weakness, leading to overconfidence and arrogance. Successful and derailed executives also differed in the way they managed hardship and mistakes. Those executives who were successful overwhelmingly handled failure with poise and grace. They admitted mistakes, accepted responsibility, and then acted to correct the problems. In contrast, leaders who derailed tended to be defensive about their failure, attempting to keep it undercover while they fixed it, or they tended to blame others. Their unwillingness and/or inability to learn from experience appeared to be the major reason why the executives derailed.

The popular literature reveals similar stories of failed leaders. In his book, *Why Smart Executives Fail*, Sydney Finkelstein (2003, p. 238) focused on a specialized subset of derailed executives—CEOs. He summarized the findings in terms of "the seven habits of spectacularly unsuccessful people." A few of the habits are directly related to learning agility, such as having all the answers and relying on what worked for them in the past. Recently, Goldsmith and Reiter (2007) advised executives "what got you here won't get you there." To continue down the path of success, successful leaders need to change, adapt, grow, and develop.

Learning Agility: What Is It? How Do We Define It?

Learning agility can be defined as the ability to learn from experience, and subsequently apply that learning to perform successfully under new or first-time conditions. Highly learning-agile individuals learn the right lessons from experience and apply those learnings to new situations (Lombardo & Eichinger, 2000). Learning agility is an important element of potential. Our research indicates that those individuals with greater learning agility are significantly more successful *after* they are promoted than others.

Learning agility is different from intelligence or simply "being smart" (Eichinger & Lombardo, 2004; Sternberg et al., 1995). An individual's intelligence refers to his or her general mental capability and encompasses many related abilities such as the capacity to reason, plan, solve problems, and think abstractly. Intelligence often is measured in terms of IQ ("Intelligence Quotient"). Being smart clearly does not guarantee managerial success (Hogan & Kaiser, 2005).

The concept that leaders need to be learning agile has been broadly recognized and accepted in the management field (see Kaiser, 2008; Kaiser, Lindberg, & Craig, 2007; Spreitzer, McCall, & Mahoney, 1997). People who are highly agile continuously seek out new challenges, actively seek feedback from others to grow and develop, tend to self-reflect, and evaluate their experiences and draw practical conclusions. Although intelligence impacts the ability to learn from a traditional perspective, individuals who are learning agile tend to be active, continuous learners throughout their lifetime. Table 1 distinguishes between traditional learners and active learners.

TABLE 1 – CHARACTERISTICS OF TRADITIONAL AND ACTIVE LEARNERS

Traditional Learners	Active Learners
■ High intellect	■ Street smarts
■ High grades, GPA, class rank	■ High initiative and motivation
■ Score well on tests (e.g., ACT, GRE)	■ Intellectually flexible
	■ High conceptual complexity
■ High functional/technical skills	■ Very broad thinkers
■ High verbal and analytical skills	■ Highly curious—why and how
■ Linear problem solver	■ High self-awareness
■ May or may not be self-aware	

A key reason managerial transitions are challenging—and developmental—is due to the fact that individuals are faced with novel situations, rendering existing routines and leadership behaviors inadequate. It requires the flexibility to learn new ways of coping with unforeseen problems and opportunities (McCauley, Ruderman, Ohlott, & Morrow, 1994; De Meuse, 2008). Individuals who can't let go of old patterns of behavior or who do not recognize the nuances in different situations tend to fail. To summarize McCall et al. (1988) and the book *Lessons of Experience*:

The glaring difference between successful people and those whose careers falter... is their ability to wrest meaning from experience (that is the essence of learning agility).

Research has indicated that individuals high on learning agility excel in the following four areas:

1. **Mental Agility:** They are excellent critical thinkers who are comfortable with complexity and ambiguity, examine problems carefully, and make fresh connections. These individuals can clearly explain their logic and thinking to others.

2. **People Agility:** They know themselves very well and can readily deal with a wide variety of people and tough situations. They are cool and resilient under the pressures of change.

3. **Change Agility:** They are curious, like to experiment, and can effectively deal with the discomfort of change. These individuals have a passion for ideas and are highly interested in continuous improvement.

4. **Results Agility:** They deliver results in first-time situations by inspiring teams and have significant presence. They exhibit the sort of presence that builds confidence in themselves and others.

Table 2 presents some key characteristics of highly agile learners for each of the above areas.

TABLE 2 – KEY CHARACTERISTICS OF HIGHLY AGILE LEARNERS

Area of Learning Agility	Characteristic
Mental Agility	■ Curious ■ Gets to root causes ■ Comfortable with ambiguity and complexity ■ Finds parallels and contrasts easily ■ Questions conventional wisdom ■ Finds solutions to *tough* problems ■ Reads broadly and has wide interests
People Agility	■ Open-minded and tolerant ■ Self-aware ■ Comfortable with diversity and differences of opinion ■ Can play many roles simultaneously ■ Understands others ■ Relishes helping others succeed ■ Politically agile ■ Deals with conflict constructively ■ Very skilled communicator
Change Agility	■ Loves tinkering and trying new things ■ Easily accepts challenges ■ Accepts responsibility and accountability ■ Introduces new slants on old ideas
Results Agility	■ Builds high-performance teams ■ Can pull off things against the odds ■ Has tremendous drive to accomplish tasks ■ Very flexible and adaptable ■ Has significant personal presence

Understanding Learning Agility in the Broader Context of Leadership

In general, leadership has been one of the most popular topics in management and industrial/organizational psychology since the beginning of the study of organizations. A recent Google search of the word "leadership" yielded 154,000,000 entries. When Stogdill edited his first comprehensive handbook of leadership in 1974, 3,000 references on leadership were listed.

Just 16 years later, the third edition of this handbook contained nearly 7,500 citations (Bass, 1990). Although a comprehensive review of the leadership literature is beyond the scope of this chapter, we examine some of the key theories and review how they relate to learning agility and the development of leadership in this section.

"GREAT MAN THEORY" OR TRAIT THEORY OF LEADERSHIP

Sir Francis Galton was one of the first scholars to apply the phrase "nature versus nurture" to the question of whether human ability was hereditary. He pioneered the quantitative analysis of leadership, describing it in detail in his 1869 book entitled *Hereditary Genius*. Galton argued that the personal qualities defining effective leadership were naturally endowed, passed on genetically from generation to generation. Gradually, this approach to leadership became known as the "Great Man Theory," because researchers attempted to identify the key leadership traits that characterized great leaders throughout history (at that time, all were thought to be men). For illustration, the Victorian-era historian Thomas Carlyle commented that "the history of the world was the biography of great men" (1907, p. 18).

Cowley (1931, p. 144) contended that "the approach to the study of leadership has usually been and perhaps always must be through the study of traits." Some of the most common traits that have been thought to be associated with effective leadership include intelligence, motivation, initiative, emotional stability, persistence, self-confidence, masculinity, and dominance (George & Jones, 2007). If one subscribes to this theoretical approach to leadership, the implication is that leadership is immutable. We are born, or not born, a leader. Hence, the implication is that leadership is not amenable to developmental interventions. Learning agility becomes irrelevant, because individuals who supposedly were born leaders would be promoted into executive positions.

SITUATIONAL AND CONTINGENCY THEORY OF LEADERSHIP

The nature or trait perspective prevailed in leadership research until the late-1940s and early-1950s. At that time, the pendulum swung to the "nurture" side of leadership. The rejection of the trait explanation of leadership emergence and effectiveness by psychologists can be attributed primarily to the findings of two types of studies (Kenny & Zaccaro, 1983). First, reviews of the trait leadership research failed to find consistent associations between traits and leadership (Mann, 1959; Stogdill, 1948). For instance, sometimes height (or extraversion or age) was found to be related to leadership success and sometimes it wasn't. A second type of research used "rotation designs" to examine trait theory. Rotation designs are based on the premise that if leadership is a function of the unique personal qualities of a leader, the same person should emerge as a leader when aspects of the situation are varied. To the contrary, if leadership is a function of either situational factors or of an interaction between qualities of the leader and the environment, varying situational factors should change who emerges as a leader. The series of rotation design studies reported that leadership emergence varied greatly across group situations. These findings led Barnlund (1962) to conclude that leadership depended *not* on individual traits but rather on situational variables.

The situational view of leadership evolved into the development of various contingency theories of leadership. Fred Fiedler was the first researcher to propose a situational theory (see Fiedler, 1967). In his Contingency Model of Leadership Effectiveness, he posited eight classifications of situational favorability. Depending upon the degree of situational favorableness, a different style of leadership was needed. House (1971) proposed another contingency approach to leadership called Path-Goal Theory. According to this theory, leaders are primarily responsible for helping followers (i.e., their direct reports) develop behaviors that will enable them to reach their goals or desired outcomes. Leader behavior will be effective to the extent that it helps direct reports cope with environmental uncertainty, threats from others, and sources of frustration on the job. Vroom and Yetton (1973) also developed a contingency theory of leadership. In their Normative Model of Leadership, they devised a series of questions that the manager should ask when leading employees. This model specifies that the degree of follower participation in leader decision making is contingent on the nature of the problem to be solved, as well as the context in which the decision is to be made. The most recent contingency approach is the Leader-Member Exchange Theory of Leadership (Liden & Graen, 1980). This theory focuses on the dyadic nature of the relationship between a leader and the followers, and how this relationship affects the leadership process.

In sum, all the situational and contingency theories of leadership suggest that there are many appropriate ways to lead or styles of leadership. Individuals can be leaders in one situation but not necessarily in others. The rejection of trait leadership is fairly widespread today. The situational view of leadership has dominated the leadership literature from the 1950s through today (Zaccaro, 2007). Most importantly, the debunking of the trait approach has significant implications for the development of leaders. Researchers who subscribe to situational theories agree that leadership can be learned and by extension that individuals can be groomed to assume higher levels of organizational leadership. This point underscores the importance and relevance of learning agility.

The finding that leaders can—and need to—vary their leadership depending on the situation becomes very apparent as they march up the organizational ladder. Scholars have realized for a long time that leader performance requirements change as one moves up in an organization. For example, Jacobs and Jaques (1987) identified three sets of leadership skills: (1) technical, (2) interpersonal, and (3) conceptual. As an individual gets promoted up the organizational hierarchy, leadership requires increasing amounts of interpersonal and conceptual skills and less and less technical skills.

The concept that ascending the organizational levels demands different and more complex leadership skills has been popularized in the practitioner world by Charan, Drotter, and Noel (2000). In their book entitled *The Leadership Pipeline*, Charan and his colleagues articulated a six-passage model of leadership development. This model defines the crucial skills for successful management transitions from the bottom of an organization (managing oneself) to the top (managing the enterprise). Each of the six management transitions in this model involves a major change of job requirements—demanding new skills, time applications, and work values. For instance, new and young employees usually spend their first few years in a company as individual contributors. They perform assigned work within given time frames. The important skills are primarily functional and technically related. When promoted to first-level supervisors, individuals need to learn how to reallocate their time so they can help other employees perform effectively. They must learn to value managerial work and believe that making time for others, planning, coordinating, and coaching are imperative in their new role. Using a large database from a 360° assessment administered in dozens of organizations, Dai, Tang, and De Meuse (2008) empirically tested and verified the pipeline model of leadership skill requirements across organizational levels (also see Lombardo & Eichinger, 2003). Thus, the concept of learning agility is tantamount to the concept of the leadership pipeline.

Learning Agility: Using the eChoices™ Online Survey to Measure It

The eChoices™ Online Survey measures four different Factors of Learning Agility in an 81-Item survey. In total, 27 Dimensions of Learning Agility are assessed. Although each Dimension is measured by three distinct survey items, not all the Factors measure the same number of Dimensions. For example, there are 11 Dimensions in the People Agility Factor; whereas, only 4 Dimensions are in the Results Agility Factor (see table 3). Details of the development of the eChoices™ Online Survey and its validity and reliability can be found in Lombardo and Eichinger (2000) and Eichinger and Lombardo (2004), as well as in the Choices Architect® Technical Manual (2010).

TABLE 3 – FACTORS AND DIMENSIONS OF LEARNING AGILITY

Factor	Dimension
Factor I – Mental Agility	1. Broad Scanner
	2. Complexity
	3. Connector
	4. Critical Thinker
	5. Easy Shifter
	6. Essence
	7. Inquisitive
	8. Solution Finder
Factor II – People Agility	9. Agile Communicator
	10. Conflict Manager
	11. Cool Transactor
	12. Helps Others Succeed
	13. Light Touch
	14. Open Minded
	15. People Smart
	16. Personal Learner
	17. Responds to Feedback
	18. Role Flexibility
	19. Self-Aware
Factor III – Change Agility	20. Experimenter
	21. Innovation Manager
	22. Taking the Heat
	23. Visioning
Factor IV – Results Agility	24. Inspires Others
	25. Delivers Results
	26. Drive
	27. Presence

Research has consistently found that learning agility as measured by Choices Architect® significantly predicts job performance following a promotion (Lombardo & Eichinger, 2000). Further, research indicates that learning agility is unrelated to a manager's IQ or personality and provides incremental validity over these other variables (Connolly & Viswesvaran, 2002). During the past 10 years, thousands of employees have been assessed using the eChoices™ Online Survey. A summary of key research findings is highlighted in the following paragraphs.

- Overall, learning agility has been found to have a normal distribution in the employee population (De Meuse, Dai, Hallenbeck, & Tang, 2008). Because companies typically administer a learning agility assessment to a selective group of (high potential) employees, a skewed distribution typically is found. The distribution has a preponderance of high mean scores. When administered to a *non*-selective group of employees, a normal distribution of learning agility scores was observed. The norms were similar to the ones reported by the instrument developer.

- In general, learning agility scores are unrelated to leader gender (De Meuse et al., 2008; Lombardo & Eichinger, 2003). However, as expected, females scored slightly higher than males on the subscale People Agility. This finding is consistent with the literature, in that females appear to be more attuned to others, learn more from others, and have more versatile interpersonal skills on average than do men. Overall, there were no statistically significant differences between male and female mean scores on *overall* learning agility.

- Learning agility generally is unrelated to age (De Meuse et al., 2008). There is some evidence that younger individuals tend to score slightly higher than older ones on the Change Agility subscale (Lombardo & Eichinger, 2003). However, *overall* learning agility mean scores were not statistically different across age groups.

- There also is no evidence suggesting significant ethnicity-related differences on learning agility as assessed by the eChoices™ Online Survey (Church & Desrosiers, 2006; De Meuse et al., 2008).

- Data obtained from different regions of the world—North America, South America, Europe, Asia, Australia/New Zealand—reveal that the eChoices™ Online Survey is a reliable instrument for measuring learning agility. Cronbach alpha reliability coefficients for the overall scale and each of the four subscales exceeded 0.85 in all five of the above global regions (De Meuse, 2008).

- In general, people tend to score relatively higher on Results Agility and Mental Agility than on People Agility and Change Agility (Lombardo &

Eichinger, 2003). This scoring pattern is consistent across the five international regions investigated (De Meuse, 2008).

■ Individuals generally lack awareness of the extent of their learning agility (De Meuse et al., 2008). When we placed employees into the following three groups—high potential, middle potential, and low potential—and then compared their self-ratings with others' ratings, we observed that individuals in the *low* potential group tend to *overrate* themselves. In contrast, individuals in the *high* potential group tend to *underrate* themselves. This pattern of self-other agreement is consistent with the findings on other multi-source assessments (Atwater & Yammarino, 1992; Eichinger & Lombardo, 2004).

■ One Fortune 500 special materials company identified approximately 100 "high potentials" through a series of talent review sessions. Subsequently, these employees were administered the eChoices™ Online Survey. Based on the survey, nearly 70% of them were classified as "high potentials," and the remaining employees all had scores above the population mean (De Meuse et al., 2008). Thus, scores on the eChoices™ Online Survey were highly related to an independent assessment of high potential.

The Development of Tomorrow's Leaders: The Development of Learning Agility

Obviously, not all individuals are successful when promoted. Research consistently indicates that certain types of individuals are more likely than others to move into senior positions (Mumford et al., 2000). As suggested by Charan et al. (2000), the passage from lower position levels to higher levels not only requires developing new skills, it also demands that leaders break old behavioral habits and accept new values that may be contradictory with previous ones. Learning agility appears to be a prerequisite for the successful progression up the leadership pipeline.

The opportunity to provide developmental experiences is a key component of any organization's talent management strategy. Who an organization places in these special developmental job assignments is particularly important. Likely, not all individuals will derive equal benefit. We suggest that individuals who are learning agile will gain the most from these assignments. Such individuals will obtain valuable lessons that can help propel them to future promotions.

Table 4 presents a matrix suggesting who probably will derive the most benefits from an enriched exposure of job duties and responsibilities. While all employees should be trained and developed, we contend that those unique job assignments which are diverse and challenging (Cell 4) be reserved for the high-learning-agile employees. Organizationally, this candidate is more likely to be successful than the non-learning-agile one. Individually, the candidate is more likely to learn vital skills, make key contacts, and obtain the necessary experience to perform successfully when promoted than another individual. Other highly learning-agile individuals with special developmental needs can be slotted into specific job assignments that target growth opportunities (Cell 3).

On the other hand, those individuals who are low on learning agility can be selectively placed in Cells 1 or 2, depending upon the availability of job assignments, the requirements of the organization, and the unique developmental needs of the candidate. Such an approach to aligning organizational developmental opportunities to the learning agility of individuals in the workforce enables an organization to systematically develop the next generation of leaders.

TABLE 4 – DEVELOPING TOMORROW'S LEADERS

JOB EXPERIENCES

	Specific and Targeted	Many and Diverse
High	3	4
Low	1	2

LEARNING AGILITY

It is clear that companies with best-in-class leadership development programs employ a structured process for assessing and identifying high potentials (Hewitt Associates, 2005; SHRM, 2006). Standardized high potential assessment and identification appears particularly important for multi-national companies where integrated approaches are a prerequisite to the building of global HR systems (Howard, 2009; Ryan, Wiechmann, & Hemingway, 2003). Once an individual is identified as a high potential talent, a careful, long-range series of job assignments is scheduled to maximize development.

Given the importance of learning agility to leadership effectiveness, a frequently asked question is, "Can we develop a manager's learning agility?" We believe that people can increase their learning agility through systematic and persistent efforts. (In fact, each of the following chapters in this book provides specific developmental activities to enhance individuals' learning agility.) Organizational leaders should recognize that research suggests employees are much more willing to challenge themselves and take risks when the company's culture fosters such a learning orientation (Senge, 2006). A learning culture encourages employees to share information, provide feedback to each other, and try innovative solutions. Consequently, organizations must establish a culture that encourages such behaviors (Ruyle, Eichinger, & De Meuse, 2009). The development of employees' learning ability doesn't happen coincidentally. Learning and development is less likely to occur when the organizational environment does not support it.

The development of learning agility also requires individuals themselves to break from habitual behavioral patterns at work. Complacency and comfortable work routines need to be avoided (Hooijberg & Quinn, 1992). Individuals must challenge and stretch themselves. New job behaviors need to be enacted. Once change is instilled as a common workplace occurrence on the job, the confidence and ability to accept new challenges increases. Development occurs. Research suggests that executives learn most from hardship—job assignments at which they fail or perform poorly (Lombardo & Eichinger, 2004; McCall et al., 1988). Such incidents require individuals to be resilient, possessing the ability to manage and deal with stress effectively. If they do not, they will react by resisting, withdrawing, or burning out. Researchers in management transition and cross-cultural assignment have observed that emotional resilience is one of the critical success factors (Stahl & Caligiuri, 2005). Emotional resilience seems to be an important component of learning agility. For learning agility to develop, it seems reasonable that individuals will need to improve their emotional resilience.

Concluding Remarks

Ever since the "war for talent" was popularized by the 1997 McKinsey report, the concept of identifying and managing high potentials has become increasingly important for organizations. More than a decade later, the war for talent has not ended. If anything, it is escalating! The development of the next generation of leaders can't be overstated. Perhaps, we should ask what percentage of *your* senior executives are promoted internally. Pharmacy giant Medco fills nearly 80% of vice president and higher positions with internal candidates (Donlon, 2009). One of the hallmarks of 3M's culture is to view virtually every employee as a potential leader. Fully, 73% of senior executives and HR leaders indicate that the urgency to develop leaders in their organizations has increased during the past three years (Donlon, 2009).

One of the tremendous advantages of using a tool like the eChoices™ Online Survey is that it provides an independent, quantifiable assessment of an individual's potential. It provides management an objective measure of the likelihood of success if promoted. As a recent *BusinessWeek* poll documented, individuals can't be depended upon to provide an accurate assessment of themselves. In the poll, 90% of the 2,000 executives who were asked claimed that they were in the top 10% of talent in their respective organizations (Coy, 2007). By the same token, potential needs to be determined independent of the individual's self-perception. In addition, the separate Dimension scores on the eChoices™ Online Survey enable the development of specific individual action plans to enhance the learning agility of one's workforce.

More than ever, organizations today require leaders (indeed, all employees) who are open to change, flexible, and willing to continuously learn, grow, and evolve. They need leaders who thrive on new challenges and experiences. Leaders who possess great people skills, a high tolerance for ambiguity, and vision and innovation. In short, leaders who are learning agile.

> *If you want one year of prosperity, grow grain.*
> *If you want 10 years of prosperity, grow trees.*
> *If you want 100 years of prosperity, grow people.*
> – Another Chinese proverb

References

Atwater, L. E., & Yammarino, F. J. (1992). Does self-other agreement on leadership perceptions moderate the validity of leadership and performance predictions? *Personnel Psychology, 45,* 41-164.

Barnlund, D. C. (1962). Consistency of emergent leadership in groups with changing tasks and members. *Speech Monographs, 29,* 45-52.

Bass, B. M. (1990). *Bass and Stogdill's handbook of leadership: Theory, research, and managerial applications* (3rd ed.). New York, NY: Free Press.

Bennis, W. G., & Thomas, R. J. (2002). *Geeks & geezers: How era, values, and defining moments shape leaders.* Boston, MA: Harvard Business School Press.

Blanchard, K. (2007). Top challenges. *Leadership Excellence, 24*(6), p. 4.

Bray, D., Campbell, R., & Grant, D. (1974). *Formative years in business: A long-term AT&T study of managerial lives.* New York, NY: Wiley.

Carlyle, T. (1907). *On heroes, hero-worship, and the heroic in history.* Boston, MA: Houghton-Mifflin.

Charan, R. (2005). Ending the CEO succession crisis. *Harvard Business Review, 83*(2), 72-81.

Charan, R., Drotter, S., & Noel, J. (2000). *The leadership pipeline: How to build the leadership powered company.* San Francisco, CA: Jossey-Bass.

Choices Architect® Technical Manual. (2010). Minneapolis, MN: Lominger International: A Korn/Ferry Company.

Church, A. H., & Desrosiers, E. I. (2006). *Talent management: Will the high potentials please stand up?* Symposium presented at the Annual Conference for the Society for Industrial and Organizational Psychology, Dallas.

Connolly, J. A., & Viswesvaran, C. (2002). *Assessing the construct validity of a measure of learning agility.* Paper presented at the Annual Conference of the Society for Industrial and Organizational Psychology, Toronto.

Corporate Leadership Council. (2005). *Realizing the full potential of rising talent.* Washington, DC: Corporate Executive Board.

Cowley, W. H. (1931). Three distinctions in the study of leaders. *Journal of Applied Psychology, 4,* 73-87.

Coy, P. (2007, August 20). Ten years from now. *BusinessWeek, 4047,* p. 42.

Dai, G., Tang, K., & De Meuse, K. P. (2008). *Leadership competencies across position levels: A test of the pipeline model.* Paper presented at the Annual Conference for the Society for Industrial and Organizational Psychology, San Francisco.

De Meuse, K. P. (2008). *Learning agility: A new construct whose time has come.* In R. B. Kaiser (Chair), *The importance, assessment, and development of flexible leadership.* Symposium presented at the Annual Conference for the Society for Industrial and Organizational Psychology, San Francisco.

De Meuse, K. P., Dai, G., Hallenbeck, G., & Tang, K. (2008). *Global talent management: Using learning agility to identify high potentials around the world.* Los Angeles: Korn/Ferry Institute.

Donlon, J. P. (2009, January/February). Best companies for leaders. *Chief Executive.net Magazine.* Retrieved from http://www.chiefexecutive.net/ ME2/dirmod.asp?sid=&nm=&type=Publishing&mod=Publications%3 A%3AArticle&mid=8F3A7027421841978F18BE895F87F791&tier=4&id= BF3221D721F74109BD2FA95B404E4AC6 [Search: Donlon. Best Companies for Leaders. Chief Executive.net Magazine].

Dychtwald, K., Erickson, T. J., & Morison, R. (2006). *Workforce crisis: How to beat the coming shortage of skills and talent.* Boston, MA: Harvard Business School Press.

Eichinger, R. W., & Lombardo, M. M. (2004). Patterns of rater accuracy in 360-degree feedback. *Human Resource Planning, 27*(4), 23-25.

Fiedler, F. E. (1967). *A theory of leadership effectiveness.* New York, NY: McGraw-Hill.

Finkelstein, S. (2003). *Why smart executives fail: And what you can learn from their mistakes.* New York, NY: Portfolio.

Galton, F. (1869). *Hereditary genius.* New York, NY: Appleton.

Gehler, C. P. (2005). *Agile leaders, agile institutions: Educating adaptive and innovative leaders for today and tomorrow.* Carlisle, PA: U. S. Army War College, Special Studies Institute.

George, J. M., & Jones, G. R. (2007). *Understanding and managing organizational behavior* (5th ed.). Upper Saddle River, NJ: Prentice-Hall.

Goldsmith, M., & Reiter, M. (2007). *What got you here won't get you there: How successful people become even more successful.* New York, NY: Hyperion.

Hewitt Associates. (2005). The top companies for leaders. *Journal of the Human Resource Planning Society, 28*(3), 18-23.

Hogan, R., & Kaiser, R. B. (2005). What we know about leadership. *Review of General Psychology, 9,* 169-180.

Hooijberg, R., & Quinn, R. E. (1992). Behavioral complexity and the development of effective managerial leaders. In R. L. Philips, & J. G. Hunt (Eds.), *Strategic management: A multi-organizational-level perspective* (pp.161-176). New York, NY: Quorum.

House, R. J. (1971). A path goal theory of leader effectiveness. *Administrative Science Quarterly, 16,* 321-339.

Howard, A. (2009). *Global leader SOS: Can multinational leadership skills be developed?* Symposium presented at the Annual Society for Industrial and Organizational Psychology Conference, New Orleans.

Howard, A., & Bray, D. (1988). *Managerial lives in transition: Advancing age and changing times.* New York, NY: Guilford Press.

Jacobs, T. O., & Jaques, E. (1987). Leadership in complex systems. In J. Zeidner (Ed.), *Human productivity enhancement* (Vol. 2, pp. 7-65). New York, NY: Praeger.

Jerusalim, R. S., & Hausdorf, P. A. (2007). Managers' justice perceptions of high potential identification practices. *Journal of Management Development, 26,* 933-950.

Kaiser, R. B. (2008). *The importance, assessment, and development of flexible leadership.* Symposium presented at the Annual Conference for the Society for Industrial and Organizational Psychology, San Francisco.

Kaiser, R. B., Lindberg, J. T., & Craig, S. B. (2007). Assessing the flexibility of managers: A comparison of methods. *International Journal of Selection and Assessment, 15*(1), 40-55.

Kenny, D. A., & Zaccaro, S. J. (1983). An estimate of variance due to traits in leadership. *Journal of Applied Psychology, 68,* 678-685.

Liden, R. C., & Graen, G. (1980). Generalizability of the vertical dyad linkage model of leadership. *Academy of Management Journal, 23,* 451-465.

Lombardo, M. M., & Eichinger, R. W. (1989). *Preventing derailment: What to do before it's too late.* Greensboro, NC: Center for Creative Leadership.

Lombardo, M. M., & Eichinger, R. W. (2000). High potentials as high learners. *Human Resource Management, 39,* 321-330.

Lombardo, M. M., & Eichinger, R. W. (2003). *The Choices Architect® user's manual.* Minneapolis, MN: Lominger International: A Korn/Ferry Company.

Lombardo, M. M., & Eichinger, R. W. (2004). *The leadership machine.* Minneapolis, MN: Lominger International: A Korn/Ferry Company.

Lombardo, M. M., Ruderman, M. N., & McCauley, C. D. (1988). Explanations of success and derailment in upper-level management positions. *Journal of Business and Psychology, 2*, 199-216.

Mann, R. D. (1959). A review of the relationship between personality and performance in small groups. *Psychological Bulletin, 56*, 241-270.

McCall, M. W., Jr., & Hollenbeck, G. P. (2002). *Developing global executives.* Boston, MA: Harvard Business School Press.

McCall, M. W., Jr., & Lombardo, M. M. (1983). What makes a top executive? *Psychology Today, 17*(2), 26-31.

McCall, M. W., Jr., Lombardo, M. M., & Morrison, A. M. (1988). *The lessons of experience: How successful executives develop on the job.* Lexington, MA: Lexington Books.

McCauley, C. D., Ruderman, M. N., Ohlott, P. J., & Morrow, J. E. (1994). Assessing the developmental components of managerial jobs. *Journal of Applied Psychology, 79*, 544-560.

Morrison, A., White, R., & Van Velsor, E. (1994). *Breaking the glass ceiling: Can women reach the top of America's largest corporations?* (Updated ed.). New York, NY: Basic Books.

Mueller-Hanson, R. A., White, S. S., Dorsey, D. W., & Pulakos, E. D. (2005). *Training adaptable leaders: Lessons from research and practice* (Research Report 1844). U. S. Army Research Institute for the Behavioral and Social Sciences. Arlington, VA: Personnel Decisions Research Institute.

Mumford, M. D., Zaccaro, S. J., Johnson, J. F., Diana, M., Gilbert, J. A., & Threlfall, K. V. (2000). Patterns of leader characteristics: Implications for performance and development. *The Leadership Quarterly, 11*(1), 115-133.

Ruyle, K. E., Eichinger, R. W., & De Meuse, K. P. (2009). *FYI for talent engagement: Drivers of best practice for managers and business leaders.* Minneapolis, MN: Lominger International: A Korn/Ferry Company.

Ryan, A. M., Wiechmann, D., & Hemingway, M. (2003). Designing and implementing global staffing systems: Part II – Best practices. *Human Resource Management, 42*(1), 85-94.

Senge, P. M. (2006). *The fifth discipline: The art & practice of the learning organization* (Rev. ed.). London: Century Business.

SHRM. (2006). *2006 Succession planning: Survey report.* Alexandria, VA: Society for Human Resource Management.

Spreitzer, G. M., McCall, M. W., Jr., & Mahoney, J. D. (1997). Early identification of international executive potential. *Journal of Applied Psychology, 82*(1), 6-29.

Stahl, G., & Caligiuri, P. M. (2005). The relationship between expatriate coping strategies and expatriate adjustment. *Journal of Applied Psychology, 90*(4), 603-616.

Sternberg, R. J. (1985). *Beyond IQ: Toward a triarchic theory of intelligence.* New York, NY: Cambridge University Press.

Sternberg, R. J. (1997). *Successful intelligence: How practical and creative intelligence determine success in life.* New York, NY: Plume.

Sternberg, R. J., Wagner, R. K., Williams, W. M., & Horvath, J. A. (1995). Testing common sense. *American Psychologist, 50*(11), 912-927.

Stogdill, R. M. (1948). Personal factors associated with leadership: A survey of the literature. *Journal of Psychology, 25*, 35-71.

Stogdill, R. M. (1974). *Handbook of leadership.* New York, NY: Free Press.

Van Velsor, E., & Leslie, J. B. (1995). Why executives derail: Perspectives across time and cultures. *Academy of Management Review, 9*(4), 62-72.

Vroom, V. H., & Yetton, P. W. (1973). *Leadership and decision-making.* Pittsburgh: University of Pittsburgh Press.

Wells, S. J. (2003). Who's next: Creating a formal program for developing new leaders can pay huge dividends, but many firms aren't reaping those rewards. *HR Magazine, 48*(11), 44-64.

Wong, L. (2004). *Developing adaptive leaders: The crucible experience of Operation Iraqi Freedom.* Carlisle, PA: U. S. Army War College, Special Studies Institute.

Zaccaro, S. J. (2007). Trait-based perspectives of leadership. *American Psychologist, 62*(1), 6-16.

Factor : I
Mental Agility

High
People high on this Factor are oriented toward newness and complexity and are described as mentally quick. They are seen as curious and inquisitive. They like to delve deeply into problems, thoroughly analyzing them through contrasts, parallels, and searching for meaning. They can get to the essence of issues better than most others can. Additionally, they can help other people think things through.

Low
People low on this Factor may have gotten stale. They may be caught in present paradigms, may be uncomfortable with change, ambiguity, and things that are messy and uncertain. Being oriented to known solutions, they may hop from solution to solution when a nasty problem appears rather than reexamining the issue for a fresh perspective. As such, they probably focus on **what**, not **why and how**, and don't search either their personal history or relevant parallels to a great degree. They may have trouble explaining how they arrived at a position and, as a consequence, might appear biased, non-objective, or even arbitrary in their positions and solutions. They may not be able to articulate the positions of others.

Some Causes
- ☐ Arrogant
- ☐ Doesn't listen
- ☐ Impatient
- ☐ Inconsistent
- ☐ Low comfort with uncertainty
- ☐ Mentally lazy
- ☐ Narrow background
- ☐ Not orderly
- ☐ Opinionated
- ☐ Overly biased against others
- ☐ Relies on the past
- ☐ Too focused
- ☐ Too rigid/stuck in their ways
- ☐ Too specialized

1

FACTOR I: MENTAL AGILITY

Dimension 1
Broad Scanner

The beginning of knowledge is the discovery of something we do not understand.
Frank Herbert, Jr. – U. S. author

Skilled
Very knowledgeable on a host of work and non-work topics.

Unskilled
May use limited sources or limited media for knowledge.

Items
- ☐ 1. Reads broadly.
- ☐ 28. Uses history and biography to find common truths, rules, and how things work.
- ☐ 55. Knows a lot about many work and non-work topics.

Leadership Architect® Competencies Most Associated with This Dimension

Strong
- ☐ 32. Learning on the Fly
- ☐ 46. Perspective

Moderate
- ☐ 2. *Dealing with* Ambiguity
- ☐ 51. Problem Solving
- ☐ 62. Time Management

Light
- ☐ 33. Listening
- ☐ 52. Process Management
- ☐ 54. Self-Development

Some Causes

☐ Doesn't take time to learn
☐ Doesn't value information not needed now
☐ Impatient
☐ Intimidated by information technology
☐ Life partner(s) also specialized or narrow
☐ Low curiosity
☐ Low tolerance for complexity
☐ Low tolerance for uncertainty
☐ Narrow band of friends, acquaintances
☐ Narrow or limited interests
☐ Prefers depth to broad
☐ Too busy
☐ Too specialized
☐ Uncomfortable approaching others for information

Developmental Difficulty

Easier

The Map

In several studies, those with a broad scope were more successful than those with a more narrow scope. A broad scope gives us more chances to come up with meaningful connections to our life and work, and ideas don't originate from boxes labeled "directly relevant to my life right this minute." Our minds are more flexible than this. Those with a broad view offer more.

Some Remedies and Workarounds

☐ **1. Looking for inspiration? Select a biography of a historical figure you admire but don't know much about.** What made the figure significant? What were his or her key accomplishments and contributions? What were critical lessons in his or her life? Write down five things you can emulate in your own behavior. A helpful Web site for finding biographical summaries, books, videos, etc. is www.biography.com. Additionally, they list a monthly schedule for the Biography Channel, a cable channel on the A&E Network dedicated to biography programs and specials on significant lives.

☐ **2. Need to broaden your horizons? Explore what you don't know.** Pick three books on topics you don't know much about and write down three things for each that relate to your job and life.

4

☐ 3. **Unaware of the broader business and/or cultural climate? Get a media download.** Start reading periodicals such as the *Economist, New Yorker, Atlantic, Forbes, Fortune,* and *BusinessWeek.* Keep a log of ideas you get from each.

☐ 4. **Too narrow or deep? Go remote.** Read a philosopher, a religious tract, or a book about physics written for the layperson. Ask yourself what common truths or insights you can gain about human nature, the way things work, and about yourself.

☐ 5. **Lacking a global perspective? Use the Internet to understand world events from other perspectives.** Read the Russian view of the Middle East, what drives the French economy, how Turkey controls the water supply to many countries. Use these primarily for personal perspective but secondarily for understanding differences.

☐ 6. **Focused only on your immediate work? Learn more about your business.** Talk to the people who know. Meet with the strategic planners, and read every significant document you can find about your business, it's customers and competitors. Reduce your understanding to rules of thumb and use these to image what initiatives could make a huge difference.

☐ 7. **Surrounded by people just like you? Spend time socially or at work functions (lunches, outings) with those who are broad in viewpoint and diverse in background.** Pay attention to topics they discuss that you aren't versed in. Make a point to learn or discover new information from them. Consider researching or investigating those topics afterward to learn more so that you can converse with them at the next encounter.

☐ 8. **Haven't learned anything new in a while? Seek out some exposure to the unfamiliar.** Attend broadening workshops and lectures on topics you normally don't get exposed to often.

☐ 9. *(Workaround)* **Not enough time to acquire learning? Tap directly into others' knowledge.** Seek counsel and advice from those broader than you.

☐ 10. *(Workaround)* **Prefer leveraging others' perspectives? Retain an expert.** Use an internal or external consultant to study the broadest aspects of issues and challenges you are facing and offer input you might want to consider.

1

More Help?

In addition to the 10 tips listed for this dimension, there are some tips that may apply from *FYI For Your Improvement*™. We have coded each item to about 10 tips from the *FYI* book. To use this resource, the codes below refer to the chapter and then the tip number from the *FYI* book. For example, in item 1 below, 2-3 refers to Chapter 2 – *Dealing with* Ambiguity, tip 3. If you don't have a copy of *FYI*, it is available through Lominger International at 952-345-3610 or www.lominger.com.

1. Reads broadly.

   2-3; 30-10; 46-1,2,3,5,6; 58-3,6; 118-8

28. Uses history and biography to find common truths, rules, and how things work.

   14-2; 30-10; 32-2,3; 46-1,2,3,6; 58-3,6

55. Knows a lot about many work and non-work topics.

   5-6; 9-1; 24-1; 28-10; 32-5,7; 46-5,7,8; 66-6

Jobs That Would Add Skills in This Dimension

☐ Cross-Moves – across functions/SBUs/products/services.

☐ International Assignments – where you have to make the connection between your background and this new setting.

☐ Scope (complexity) Assignments – often involving new businesses, functions to deal with. Requires making a significant transition such as to manager of managers, or functional head to general manager.

Part-Time Assignments That Would Add Skills in This Dimension

☐ Assemble a team of diverse people to accomplish a difficult task.

☐ Integrate diverse systems, processes, or procedures across decentralized and/or dispersed units.

☐ Work on a project that involves travel to places you have never been to or study issues you have never studied.

☐ Study a new trend, product, service, technique, or process you have never experienced before.

☐ Manage a project team made up of nationals from a number of countries you have not had any experience with before.

☐ Study the history of an event or an institution or country you have had no experience with before.

Knowledge has to be improved, challenged,
and increased constantly, or it vanishes.
Peter F. Drucker – U. S. writer and management consultant

Suggested Readings

Atlantic. http://www.theatlantic.com.

BusinessWeek. http://www.businessweek.com.

Collins, J. (2001). *Good to great.* New York, NY: Harper Collins.

Commentary Magazine. http://www.commentarymagazine.com.

Dixon, P. (2007). *Futurewise: The six faces of global change* (4th ed.). London: Profile Books Ltd.

Drucker, P. F. (2001). *Management challenges for the 21st century.* New York, NY: HarperBusiness.

Economist. http://www.economist.com.

Elmer, D. (2002). *Cross-cultural connections: Stepping out and fitting in around the world.* Downers Grove, IL: Inter Varsity Press.

Fast Company. http://www.fastcompany.com.

Friedman, T. L. (2007). *The world is flat: A brief history of the twenty-first century.* New York, NY: Picador.

Futurist Magazine. http://www.wfs.org.

Hamel, G. (with Breen, B.). (2007). *The future of management.* Boston, MA: Harvard Business School Press.

Hamel, G., & Prahalad, C. K. (1996). *Competing for the future.* Boston, MA: Harvard Business School Press.

Harvard Business Review. http://www.hbr.harvardbusinessreview.org.

International Herald Tribune. http://www.iht.com.

Kennedy, P. M. (1987). *The rise and fall of the great powers: Economic change and military conflict from 1500 to 2000.* New York, NY: Random House.

New York Times. (2007). *The New York Times guide to essential knowledge: A desk reference for the curious mind* (2nd ed.). New York, NY: St. Martin's Press.

Oxford University Press. (2008). *The ultimate book of knowledge: Everything you need to know.* New York, NY: Oxford University Press.

Porter, M. E. (2008). *On competition: Updated and expanded edition.* Boston, MA: Harvard Business School Press.

Schultz, P. (2003). *1,000 Places to see before you die: A traveler's life list.* New York, NY: Workman Publishing Company, Inc.

Sloan Management Review. http://sloanreview.mit.edu.

Soundview Executive Book Summaries. http://www.summary.com.

FACTOR I: MENTAL AGILITY

1

Stearns, P. N. (2002). *The encyclopedia of world history: Ancient, medieval & modern.* New York, NY: Houghton Mifflin Company.

van Agtmael, A. (2007). *The emerging markets century: How a new breed of world-class companies is overtaking the world.* New York, NY: Free Press.

Wall Street Journal. http://www.wsj.com.

Dimension 2
Complexity

There is no simplistic approach to worthwhile achievement in human affairs.
William Hastie – U. S. Federal Appeals Court Judge

Skilled
Comfortable with things that don't fit; casts a broad net; doesn't try to make things simpler than they are; can pull from many sources, see the importance of many factors.

Unskilled
Prefers to keep things simple; may not have good conceptual buckets to put disparate data in; may be thrown by problems or situations that don't fit.

Items
- ☐ 2. Is intellectually quick; picks up on things in a hurry.
- ☐ 29. Can project consequences and how things are connected.
- ☐ 56. Is comfortable with complexity.

Leadership Architect® Competencies Most Associated with This Dimension

Strong
- ☐ 2. *Dealing with* Ambiguity
- ☐ 14. Creativity
- ☐ 32. Learning on the Fly
- ☐ 51. Problem Solving

Moderate
- ☐ 30. Intellectual Horsepower
- ☐ 46. Perspective
- ☐ 52. Process Management
- ☐ 58. Strategic Agility
- ☐ 61. Technical Learning

Light
- ☐ 50. Priority Setting

9

Some Causes

☐ Doesn't think beyond his/her own work/tasks
☐ Gets frustrated when he/she isn't in the know
☐ Gets stressed and overwhelmed easily
☐ Impatient
☐ Low tolerance for ambiguity and uncertainty
☐ Narrow background
☐ Not comfortable with not knowing, not answering; can't say I don't know
☐ Not strategic; doesn't anticipate outcomes
☐ Overly results driven
☐ Oversimplifies
☐ Single-tracked
☐ Slow to catch on
☐ Too specialized

Developmental Difficulty

Easier

The Map

Complexity is a part of life. And it is probably increasing, especially in the area of life and work technologies. People who offer truly simple explanations and solutions to complex problems will have had to understand its complexity first. Globalization and speed are adding to the complexity. While trying to get everything to be simple is a worthy goal, it is probably not reflective of truth.

Some Remedies and Workarounds

☐ **1. Impatient? Slow down and select the solution that fits.** Coming to quick, simple solutions is the bane of many a problem solver. Practice adding complexity and resisting the urge to just decide. To do this, ask how many elements or factors does this problem have? What is related to it? What is not related to it?

☐ **2. Overwhelmed? Put all like elements into conceptual buckets.** For example, everything to do with costing in one bucket, everything having to do with people in another. Analyze how the buckets can work together and how they work against each other. Create processes for each bucket and processes for the buckets as a whole.

☐ **3. Trouble identifying a root cause? Resist saying you know what causes a problem.** Most issues worth considering are multi-causal. Ask why or how this could be a cause to better understand the nature of the beast. What would you accept as evidence that your problem definition is

2

correct? What consequences would occur? What wouldn't occur? What are you prepared to do if your definition is incorrect?

☐ **4. Too quick to decide? Spend more time studying the problem.** If you make decisions too quickly, work to better understand your patience triggers. Is time pressure one of them? Do you make quick decisions just to check something off your list or get someone out of your hair? Analyze the factors that cause you to avoid taking the time to consider complexity, and discipline yourself to spend half your problem-solving time defining the problem and thinking about all of its elements. Even if that's only ten minutes, use five to look more thoroughly.

☐ **5. First solution not working? Take time to generate more ideas.** Since studies show that defining a problem and taking action happen almost simultaneously, you may as well load more effort on the front end. That's your best chance of a breakthrough solution. Discipline yourself to go for the second and third solution—the "what else could we do" question. Studies show the second or third solutions are often superior.

☐ **6. Missing critical information? Ask more questions.** Studies have shown that about 50% of discussions involve answers; only 7% involve probing questions. Why does that work? Why might my solution not work this time? How would I know if it did or didn't? What's least likely? What's missing from the problem?

☐ **7. *(Workaround)* Everyone looking to you for answers? Teach them to find their own.** If you have people working for you, push back on them continually coming to you for solutions. If you create an environment that encourages others to probe problems more deeply, you may be able to compensate for your own shortcomings.

☐ **8. *(Workaround)* Unfamiliar problem? Reach out for more perspective.** Ask a subject-matter expert in the area of the problem to help you define the parameters of the problem. If your experiences are narrow or unrelated to the problem, you may need to learn to ask for help to get to the right solution.

☐ **9. *(Workaround)* Common problem, yet still difficult? Get the relevant history.** Find examples of how others have approached this or similar problems.

☐ **10. *(Workaround)* Have experts close at hand? Leverage their skills.** Hire one or two people who are especially good at this and delegate the task to them. Ask for regular updates so that you learn and understand the techniques and processes they use to solve complex problems.

More Help?

In addition to the 10 tips listed for this dimension, there are some tips that may apply from *FYI For Your Improvement*™. We have coded each item to about 10 tips from the *FYI* book. To use this resource, the codes below refer to the chapter and then the tip number from the *FYI* book. For example, in item 2 below, 1-5 refers to Chapter 1 – Action Oriented, tip 5. If you don't have a copy of *FYI*, it is available through Lominger International at 952-345-3610 or www.lominger.com.

   2. Is intellectually quick; picks up on things in a hurry.

      1-5; 14-4; 16-4; 30-4; 32-1,2,3,5,9; 58-4

  29. Can project consequences and how things are connected.

      17-2,3; 32-1,2,3; 46-1,2; 58-3,4,6

  56. Is comfortable with complexity.

      2-1,2,5; 14-4; 17-3; 32-2,3; 58-4; 101-6; 118-8

Jobs That Would Add Skills in This Dimension

☐ Fix-Its/Turnarounds – requiring lots of decisions on incomplete data in a short time frame.

☐ Heavy Strategic Demands – charting new ground for products/services.

☐ Scope (complexity) Assignments – managing a high variety of activities.

Part-Time Assignments That Would Add Skills in This Dimension

☐ Relaunch an existing product/service that's not doing well.

☐ Work with a highly diverse team to accomplish a difficult task.

☐ Manage a group where they are more expert in the technology than you are.

☐ Work on a project that involves travel, benchmarking, and exploration of issues and topics you have never studied before.

☐ Work on a multi-functional team trying to solve an issue that crosses boundaries in the organization.

☐ Work on a team that has to integrate diverse systems (move from using five computer platforms into one), processes (integrating a distinct, stand-alone, quality-assurance process into a product development process), or procedures (five competency models into one) across decentralized and/or dispersed units.

☐ Do a competitive analysis of your organization's products or services or position in the marketplace, and present it to senior decision makers.

Fools ignore complexity. Pragmatists suffer it. Some can avoid it. Geniuses remove it. Simplicity does not precede complexity, but follows it.
Alan Perlis – American computer scientist

Suggested Readings

De Bono, E. (1999). *Six thinking hats* (2nd ed.). Boston, MA: Little, Brown and Co.

Dettmer, H. W. (2007). *The logic thinking process: A systems approach to complex problem solving* (2nd ed.). Milwaukee, WI: American Society for Quality, Quality Press.

Drucker, P. (2001). *Management challenges for the 21st century.* New York, NY: HarperBusiness.

Hamel, G. (with Breen, B.). (2007). *The future of management.* Boston, MA: Harvard Business School Press.

Hamel, G., & Prahalad, C. K. (1996). *Competing for the future.* Boston, MA: Harvard Business School Press.

Hurson, T. (2007). *Think better: An innovator's guide to productive thinking.* New York, NY: McGraw-Hill.

Kennedy, P. M. (1987). *The rise and fall of the great powers: Economic change and military conflict from 1500 to 2000.* New York, NY: Random House.

Lissack, M., & Roos, J. (2000). *The next common sense: The e-manager's guide to mastering complexity.* Naperville, IL: Nicholas Brealey Publishing.

Martin, R. (2007). *The opposable mind: How successful leaders win through integrative thinking.* Boston, MA: Harvard Business School Press.

Pascale, R. T., Millemann, M., & Gioja, L. (2000). *Surfing the edge of chaos: The laws of nature and the new laws of business.* New York, NY: Three Rivers Press.

Paul, R. W., & Elder, L. (2002). *Critical thinking: Tools for taking charge of your professional and personal life.* Upper Saddle River, NJ: Financial Times/Prentice Hall.

Porter, M. E. (2008). *On competition: Updated and expanded edition.* Boston, MA: Harvard Business School Press.

Prahalad, C. K., & Ramaswamy, V. (2004). *The future of competition: Co-creating unique value with customers.* Boston, MA: Harvard Business School Press.

Steger, U., Amann, W., & Maznevski, M. (Eds.). (2007). *Managing complexity in global organizations.* West Sussex, England: John Wiley & Sons.

Weick, K. E., & Sutcliffe, K. M. (2007). *Managing the unexpected: Resilient performance in an age of uncertainty* (2nd ed.). San Francisco, CA: Jossey-Bass.

Wilkinson, D. (2006). *The ambiguity advantage: What great leaders are great at.* Hampshire, England: Palgrave Macmillan.

Wind, J., Crook, C., & Gunther, R. (2004). *The power of impossible thinking: Transform the business of your life and the life of your business.* Upper Saddle River, NJ: Wharton School Publishing.

Dimension 3
Connector

*In nature we never see anything isolated, but everything in connection
with something else which is before it, beside it, under it and over it.*
Johann Wolfgang von Goethe – German playwright and novelist

Skilled

Intellectually rigorous; looks deeply at many sources, hunts for parallels, contrasts, unique combinations. Isn't afraid to go off on an intellectual tangent and take time to think through something.

Unskilled

May be intellectually lazy, think he/she already knows the answer, or even be too quick to act; may lack historical perspective, doesn't hunt for fresh views or solutions. If action oriented, this may mask dislike or disdain for detailed problem searches or looking for seemingly obscure parallels.

Items

- ☐ 3. Can point out and find parallels, perspectives, contrasts, contexts, connections, or combinations.
- ☐ 30. Uses multiple sources to get data and answers.
- ☐ 57. Is able to connect things others don't see as related.

Leadership Architect® Competencies Most Associated with This Dimension

Strong

- ☐ 2. *Dealing with* Ambiguity
- ☐ 14. Creativity
- ☐ 32. Learning on the Fly
- ☐ 46. Perspective
- ☐ 51. Problem Solving
- ☐ 52. Process Management

Moderate

- ☐ 30. Intellectual Horsepower
- ☐ 58. Strategic Agility

15

3

Light
☐ 17. Decision Quality

Some Causes
☐ Arrogant, know-it-all
☐ Cautious
☐ Impatient
☐ Intellectually lazy; doesn't apply self
☐ Intimidated by other sources
☐ Limited ways to think
☐ Low tolerance of ambiguity and uncertainty
☐ Narrow or disadvantaged background
☐ Not curious
☐ Only skims the surface
☐ Rejects speculation
☐ Relies too much on self
☐ Restrained
☐ Single-tracked
☐ Sticks with the proven
☐ Too specialized
☐ Won't admit when he/she doesn't know something

Developmental Difficulty
Moderate

The Map
Creativity is defined as connecting two knowns that were previously unconnected. If you restrict yourself to the connections you currently make, you'll only come up with breakthrough ideas by sheer chance. Things repeatedly repeat in life. Similar things happen in parallel areas of life. Almost nothing is truly new. Almost everything has already happened. You can increase your chances of success by learning from the lessons of history and making connections across usually isolated areas.

Some Remedies and Workarounds
☐ 1. **Driven by logic? Make your mind a bit sillier.** You don't have to tell anyone what you're doing. Ask what song is this problem like? Find an analogy to your problem in nature, in children's toys, in anything that has a physical structure. Silly parallels can help you create the rules of thumb for the serious ones.

☐ 2. **Difficulty seeing the possibilities? Ask what's the least likely reason for something to happen, then connect it to the most likely.** Build a scale or measure of least to most likelihoods to gauge the scenario.

☐ 3. **Trouble putting it all together? Look for anomalies, unusual facts that don't quite fit in.** Why did sales go down when they should have gone up? It could be random, but maybe not. The unusual facts can help you to determine hidden causes and effects, measures, and other helpful pieces of data.

☐ 4. **Not picking up on important patterns? Look for what was always present in a success but was never present in a failure.** Or, look for what was always present in a failure but never present in a success. What are the critical contrasts? How can they be applied to other things you encounter?

☐ 5. **Not finding solutions in your own organization? Hunt for parallels in other organizations and in remote areas totally outside your field.** By this we don't mean best practices, which come and go. Find a parallel situation to the underlying issue—for example, who has to do things really fast (Domino's, FedEx)? Who has to deal with maximum ambiguity (emergency room, a newspaper, police dispatchers)?

☐ 6. **Stuck in the present? Hunt for parallels in history.** There are always plenty of candidates. Harry Truman used the presidential archives to form what he called his "council of presidents" to see what others had done in parallel situations.

☐ 7. **Looking for inspiration? Study the biographies of three creative people without regard to their field.** See what processes they shared in common that helped them be more creative. A helpful Web site for finding biographical summaries, books, videos, etc. is www.biography.com. Additionally, they list a monthly schedule for the Biography Channel, a cable channel on the A&E Network dedicated to biography programs and specials on significant lives.

☐ 8. **(Workaround) Getting the same perspective from others? Broaden your sources.** Talk to an expert in an unrelated field or to the most iconoclastic person you know.

☐ 9. **(Workaround) Difficulty venturing beyond tried-and-true solutions? Convene a group with the widest possible variety of backgrounds.** (Yes, we mean widest. It makes no difference if they know anything about the problem.) During World War II, it was discovered that groups with maximum diversity produced the most creative solutions to problems. You're looking for fresh approaches here, not practicality. That comes later as you sift through the ideas.

☐ 10. *(Workaround)* In a creative rut? Use internal or external consultants or subject-matter experts to help move beyond the obvious and beyond what most others would come up with. Ask questions of the consultants to learn from their problem-solving techniques. How do they collect data? How do they analyze it?

More Help?

In addition to the 10 tips listed for this dimension, there are some tips that may apply from *FYI For Your Improvement*™. We have coded each item to about 10 tips from the *FYI* book. To use this resource, the codes below refer to the chapter and then the tip number from the *FYI* book. For example, in item 3 below, 17-3,5 refers to Chapter 17 – Decision Quality, tips 3 and 5. If you don't have a copy of *FYI*, it is available through Lominger International at 952-345-3610 or www.lominger.com.

3. Can point out and find parallels, perspectives, contrasts, contexts, connections, or combinations.

   17-3,5; 30-2,6; 32-1,2,3,10; 41-7; 101-3

30. Uses multiple sources to get data and answers.

   14-2,3,4; 17-3; 30-2; 32-5,7; 33-3; 41-7; 101-3

57. Is able to connect things others don't see as related.

   14-1,2,3,4; 32-1,2,3; 46-4,5,6

Jobs That Would Add Skills in This Dimension

☐ Fix-Its/Turnarounds – requiring lots of decisions on incomplete data in a short time frame.

☐ Heavy Strategic Demands – charting new ground for products/services that will require collecting and analyzing lots of data.

☐ International Assignments – where you have to make the connection between your background and this new setting.

☐ Scope (complexity) Assignments – managing a high variety of activities.

☐ Start-Ups – requiring doing first-time things drawing from diverse sources.

Part-Time Assignments That Would Add Skills in This Dimension

☐ Work with a highly diverse team to accomplish a difficult task.

☐ Relaunch an existing product/service that's not doing well.

☐ Take on a tough and undoable project where others have failed.

☐ Work on a team fixing something that has failed.

☐ Work on a team managing a significant business crisis (e.g., product scare, scandal, natural disaster, violent crime against employees, competitor significantly erodes market position).

☐ Work on a multi-functional team trying to solve an issue that crosses boundaries in the organization.

Making mental connections is our most crucial learning tool, the essence of human intelligence: to forge links; to go beyond the given; to see patterns, relationships, and context.
Marilyn Ferguson – American writer

Suggested Readings

Albrecht, K. (2007). *Practical intelligence: The art and science of common sense.* San Francisco, CA: Jossey-Bass.

De Bono, E. (1999). *Six thinking hats* (2nd ed.). Boston, MA: Little, Brown and Co.

De Bono, E. (2008). *Creativity workout: 62 Exercises to unlock your most creative ideas.* Berkeley, CA: Ulysses Press.

Drucker, P. (2001). *Management challenges for the 21st century.* New York, NY: HarperBusiness.

Grothe, M. (2008). *I never metaphor I didn't like: A comprehensive compilation of history's greatest analogies, metaphors, and similes.* New York, NY: Harper Collins.

Hamel, G., & Prahalad, C. K. (1996). *Competing for the future.* Boston, MA: Harvard Business School Press.

Hurson, T. (2007). *Think better: An innovator's guide to productive thinking.* New York, NY: McGraw-Hill.

Kennedy, P. M. (1987). *The rise and fall of the great powers: Economic change and military conflict from 1500 to 2000.* New York, NY: Random House.

Michalko, M. (2001). *Cracking creativity: The secrets of creative genius.* Berkeley, CA: Ten Speed Press.

Pink, D. H. (2006). *A whole new mind: Why right-brainers will rule the future.* New York, NY: Berkley Publishing Group.

Prahalad, C. K., & Ramaswamy, V. (2004). *The future of competition: Co-creating unique value with customers.* Boston, MA: Harvard Business School Press.

Proctor, T. (2005). *Creative problem solving for managers: Developing skills for decision making and innovation* (2nd ed.). New York, NY: Routledge.

Risby, B. (2005). *Thinking through analogies.* San Luis Obispo, CA: Dandy Lion Publications.

Root-Bernstein, M. M., & Root-Bernstein, R. S. (2001). *Sparks of genius: The thirteen tools of the world's most creative people.* New York, NY: Mariner Books.

Schmitt, B. H. (2007). *Big think strategy: How to leverage bold ideas and leave small thinking behind.* Boston, MA: Harvard Business School Press.

Sloane, P. (2006). *The leader's guide to lateral thinking skills: Unlocking the creativity and innovation in you and your team* (2nd ed.). Philadelphia: Kogan Page.

Sternberg, R. J. (2007). *Wisdom, intelligence, and creativity synthesized.* New York, NY: Cambridge University Press.

The Systems Thinker®. http://www.thesystemsthinker.com.

Von Oech, R. (2008). *A whack on the side of the head: How you can be more creative.* (Rev. ed.). Dublin: Business Plus.

Dimension 4
Critical Thinker

Skilled
Takes the time to look at and question conventional wisdom; doesn't accept much as a given; looks beyond.

Unskilled
May have trouble with ideas that don't fit, violate what's been done in the past, or are uncomfortable. May simply like the predictability of known solutions.

Items
- ☐ 4. Faces paradox; can look at ideas or solutions that violate common sense and yet might still be true.
- ☐ 31. Usually takes time to critically examine conventional wisdom and givens before moving on.
- ☐ 58. Is a good questioner of self and others.

Leadership Architect® Competencies Most Associated with This Dimension

Strong
- ☐ 41. Patience
- ☐ 46. Perspective
- ☐ 51. Problem Solving

Moderate
- ☐ 2. *Dealing with* Ambiguity
- ☐ 14. Creativity
- ☐ 33. Listening
- ☐ 40. *Dealing with* Paradox

Light
- ☐ 32. Learning on the Fly
- ☐ 52. Process Management
- ☐ 62. Time Management

Some Causes

☐ Active biases
☐ Conventional
☐ Disinterest
☐ Doesn't read people
☐ Doesn't read situations
☐ Fear of being different
☐ Impatient
☐ Low tolerance of ambiguity
☐ Narrow background
☐ Not challenged
☐ Not curious
☐ Rigid
☐ Strong beliefs
☐ Too trusting of others

Developmental Difficulty

Moderate

The Map

Do you pretty much go with your history of what has worked for you and others? Do you like predictability? Uncomfortable with odd notions? Uncomfortable with going against group opinion or prefer to decide alone? If so, you're restricting your decision-making, problem-solving flexibility. All issues and problems have some portion of uniqueness to them. Almost nothing is the same the second or third time. Question what is. Don't take things for granted.

Some Remedies and Workarounds

☐ **1. Not getting feedback? Think out loud.** Figure out what you really think by describing the issue or problem to another person. Find a solid sounding board or go to the most irreverent person you know. Look for people who will challenge your thinking and have the courage to push back.

☐ **2. Few ideas coming to the surface? Practice the rules of brainstorming in group settings.** Lots of ideas, no evaluation. Encourage any form of participation; don't restrict idea flow.

☐ **3. Missing critical information? Ask more questions.** Studies have shown that about 50% of discussions involve answers; only 7% involve probing questions. Why does that work? Why might my solution not work this time? How would I know if it did or didn't? What's least likely? What's missing from the problem?

☐ **4. Solutions not working? Write down your best solution then throw it out.** Come up with a second and a third. Now decide which one is best. Research has shown that most of the time the best answer isn't the first one you come up with.

☐ **5. Uncomfortable with ambiguity? Think small.** Make small decisions, get feedback, correct errors, get more data, move forward a bit more. Up your comfort with ambiguity by dealing with it in bite-size chunks.

☐ **6. Taking things at face value? Define the problem—don't put it in a familiar box so you can feel comfortable.** What is it and what isn't it? How many causes can you think of? Are you stating things as facts that are really your opinion? Are you generalizing from an example or two? Use patterns and themes to define problems.

☐ **7. Uncomfortable standing alone? Go against the grain.** Be able to state in a few sentences why a lone view you hold might be correct. Build a case around business or system issues; don't let it get personal. Be able to state opposing views as well as detractors can.

☐ **8. Lacking context? Evaluate your solutions by doing downstream "what if" analyses.** How does this impact other issues/people/customers/suppliers, etc.? Many times, there are unanticipated consequences to otherwise good-sounding solutions. You might be able to find and select better solutions by visualizing what would follow if your proposed solutions were implemented.

☐ **9. *(Workaround)* Too close to the problem? Find external or internal people who are by nature critical thinkers who have no stake in the issue or the answers.** Let them work on the problem before you do. Have them prepare as many alternatives that they can for you to choose from.

☐ **10. *(Workaround)* Favor a conventional viewpoint? Look at how others have approached and solved this issue or problem before you.** Or, have some staff support people research the issue or problem and urge them to find as many different and unique solutions as they can.

4

More Help?

In addition to the 10 tips listed for this dimension, there are some tips that may apply from *FYI For Your Improvement*™. We have coded each item to about 10 tips from the *FYI* book. To use this resource, the codes below refer to the chapter and then the tip number from the *FYI* book. For example, in item 4 below, 14-1,2,3,4,5 refers to Chapter 14 – Creativity, tips 1–5. If you don't have a copy of *FYI*, it is available through Lominger International at 952-345-3610 or www.lominger.com.

4. Faces paradox; can look at ideas or solutions that violate common sense and yet might still be true.

   14-1,2,3,4,5; 51-3,4; 101-2,3; 118-8

31. Usually takes time to critically examine conventional wisdom and givens before moving on.

   14-2; 51-1,2,3,4,5,8; 58-3; 101-2,6

58. Is a good questioner of self and others.

   31-2; 32-1,2,3; 33-1,2,3,4,8; 51-1

Jobs That Would Add Skills in This Dimension

☐ Heavy Strategic Demands – charting new ground for products/services.
☐ International Assignments – where you have to think through problems from a novel position and for this new setting.
☐ Scope (complexity) Assignments – managing a high variety of activities.
☐ Start-Ups – requiring doing first-time things drawing from diverse sources.

Part-Time Assignments That Would Add Skills in This Dimension

☐ Work with a highly diverse team to accomplish a difficult task.
☐ Relaunch an existing product/service that's not doing well.
☐ Take on a tough and undoable project where others have failed.
☐ Work on a team fixing something that has failed.
☐ Work on a team managing a significant business crisis (e.g., product scare, scandal, natural disaster, violent crime against employees, competitor significantly erodes market position).
☐ Prepare and present a proposal of some consequence to top management (and anticipate the questions that senior leaders will pose).

☐ Work on a team that has to integrate diverse systems (move from using five computer platforms into one), processes (integrating a distinct, stand-alone, quality-assurance process into a product development process), or procedures (five competency models into one) across decentralized and/or dispersed units.

One's first step in wisdom is to question everything—
and one's last is to come to terms with everything.
Georg Christoph Lichtenberg – German scientist and satirist

4

Suggested Readings

De Bono, E. (1999). *Six thinking hats* (2nd ed.). Boston, MA: Little, Brown and Co.

Handy, C. (1994). *The age of paradox*. Boston, MA: Harvard Business School Press.

Hurson, T. (2007). *Think better: An innovator's guide to productive thinking*. New York, NY: McGraw-Hill.

Kennedy, P. M. (1987). *The rise and fall of the great powers: Economic change and military conflict from 1500 to 2000*. New York, NY: Random House.

Martin, R. (2007). *The opposable mind: How successful leaders win through integrative thinking*. Boston, MA: Harvard Business School Press.

Moore, B. N., & Parker, R. (2008). *Critical thinking* (9th ed.). New York, NY: McGraw-Hill.

Paul, R. W., & Elder, L. (2002). *Critical thinking: Tools for taking charge of your professional and personal life*. Upper Saddle River, NJ: Financial Times/Prentice Hall.

Pfeffer, J. (2007). *What were they thinking? Unconventional wisdom about management*. Boston, MA: Harvard Business School Press.

Sloane, P. (2006). *The leader's guide to lateral thinking skills: Unlocking the creativity and innovation in you and your team* (2nd ed.). Philadelphia: Kogan Page.

Sternberg, R. J. (2007). *Wisdom, intelligence, and creativity synthesized*. New York, NY: Cambridge University Press.

The Systems Thinker®. http://www.thesystemsthinker.com.

Wilkinson, D. (2006). *The ambiguity advantage: What great leaders are great at*. Hampshire, England: Palgrave Macmillan.

Dimension 5
Easy Shifter

The quest for certainty blocks the search for meaning.
Uncertainty is the very condition to impel man to unfold his powers.
Erich Fromm – German psychoanalyst and social psychologist

Skilled
Comfortable when things are up in the air; shifts gears easily.

Unskilled
May be uncomfortable with ambiguity, or likes to stick to one action/solution rather than change courses.

Items
- ☐ 5. Easily shifts gears from one action/solution to another.
- ☐ 32. Functions as effectively under conditions of ambiguity as when things are more certain.
- ☐ 59. Is comfortable when things are ambiguous, uncertain, or up in the air.

Leadership Architect® Competencies Most Associated with This Dimension

Strong
- ☐ 2. *Dealing with* Ambiguity
- ☐ 32. Learning on the Fly
- ☐ 40. *Dealing with* Paradox

Moderate
- ☐ 11. Composure
- ☐ 39. Organizing
- ☐ 50. Priority Setting
- ☐ 51. Problem Solving

Light
- ☐ 1. Action Oriented
- ☐ 16. *Timely* Decision Making
- ☐ 46. Perspective
- ☐ 57. Standing Alone

Some Causes
- ☐ Can't multi-task
- ☐ Cautious
- ☐ Dislikes change
- ☐ Gets stressed or overwhelmed easily
- ☐ High need to close
- ☐ High need to finish
- ☐ Impatient
- ☐ Lack of composure
- ☐ Low frustration tolerance
- ☐ Low tolerance of ambiguity
- ☐ Needs to be sure and certain
- ☐ Perfectionist
- ☐ Prefers structure and control

Developmental Difficulty
Moderate

The Map
Dealing with change is synonymous with dealing with ambiguity. Some studies estimate that 90% of what managers deal with is at least somewhat ambiguous. The world is getting less and less predictable. Those more tolerant of ambiguity and uncertainty will do better. The half-life of solutions, styles, or habits is getting shorter. Nothing lasts very long. Change is what's happening. Change is uncertain.

Some Remedies and Workarounds
- ☐ **1. Uncertain about the solution? Do quick experiments.** Studies show that 80% of innovations occur in the wrong place or are created by the wrong people working on something else. Test something out, study the results, learn, do it a little better the next time.

- ☐ **2. Trouble shifting gears? Diagnose your transition trouble points.** All of us have to shift behavior each day. We act differently when things run well and when they don't. We act differently with different people. Study the transitions you make each day and write down which ones give you the most trouble and why. Are they more people-related, process-related, schedule-related, etc.?

- ☐ **3. Get stressed out easily? Devise strategies to deal with uncomfortable situations.** If you get sharp under pressure, use some humor to counter this tendency. If you're too tough on others, ask yourself how you'd like to be treated in this situation.

28

☐ 4. **Resorting to familiar habits? Use mental rehearsal for tough situations.** Learn to recognize the clues that you're about to fall back on old behavior and be ready with a fresh strategy that you have decided in advance. If you know, for example, that a solution isn't working and you're likely to be questioned about it, be ready to engage others and get the benefit of their thinking.

☐ 5. **Perfectionist? Don't try to get it totally right the first time.** If a situation is ambiguous, be incremental. Make some small decisions, get instant feedback, treat mistakes and failures as ways to learn. Focus on your third or fourth try, not the first.

☐ 6. **Have an answer or solution to most things? Hear what others have to say.** Trying to wipe out uncertainty by plucking an answer from your hat? If you jump to conclusions or dismiss others' ideas, this is probably getting you into trouble. Use gentler words, ask questions, let others talk without interruption, pause to see what others have to say.

☐ 7. **Looking for inspiration? Study the lives of people who have done well under conditions of ambiguity and uncertainty.** Read their biographies or autobiographies. What did they do under time of high chaos? A helpful Web site for finding biographical summaries, books, videos, etc. is www.biography.com. Additionally, they list a monthly schedule for the Biography Channel, a cable channel on the A&E Network dedicated to biography programs and specials on significant lives.

☐ 8. **Stuck in place while looking for direction? Trim the uncertainty.** Break it down into pieces. Nothing is really ever totally uncertain. Solve the little things and get them out of the way. Do something. Generally, little actions will trim the size of the uncertainty until is gets small enough to comfortably tackle.

☐ 9. **Need closure? Work on leaving things undone and unfinished.** Move on to something else. Take a break. Clear your head. The brain has the capacity to continue to work on the problem while you are doing something else. Many times, the solutions will occur to you when you are doing something completely different or even when you are sleeping!

☐ 10. *(Workaround)* **Not sure how to respond? Find a good model.** Pattern your response to uncertainty and ambiguity after someone around you that doesn't seem to be bothered when things are up in the air. Worry when they do; relax when they are relaxed about what is going on.

More Help?

In addition to the 10 tips listed for this dimension, there are some tips that may apply from *FYI For Your Improvement*™. We have coded each item to about 10 tips from the *FYI* book. To use this resource, the codes below refer to the chapter and then the tip number from the *FYI* book. For example, in item 5 below, 32-1,8,9 refers to Chapter 32 – Learning on the Fly, tips 1,8,9. If you don't have a copy of *FYI*, it is available through Lominger International at 952-345-3610 or www.lominger.com.

5. Easily shifts gears from one action/solution to another.

    32-1,8,9; 40-1,2,3,5,9,10; 118-8

32. Functions as effectively under conditions of ambiguity as when things are more certain.

    2-2,3,7,9; 16-4; 58-4; 101-1,2,3,6

59. Is comfortable when things are ambiguous, uncertain, or up in the air.

    2-2,3,7,9; 16-4; 58-4; 101-1,2,3,6

Jobs That Would Add Skills in This Dimension

☐ Chair of Projects/Task Forces – where the role is different than being a functional manager, with diversity in the group, with tight deadlines, and multiple constituencies.

☐ Fix-Its/Turnarounds – requiring lots of different decisions and actions in a short period of time.

☐ Scope (complexity) Assignments – managing a high variety of activities.

☐ Start-Ups – requiring doing a lot of first-time things, shifting from role to role in a very short period of time.

Part-Time Assignments That Would Add Skills in This Dimension

☐ Work on a team fixing something that has failed.

☐ Take on a tough and undoable project where others have failed.

☐ Work with a highly diverse team to accomplish a difficult task.

☐ Plan a new site for a building or installation (plant, field office, headquarters, etc.).

☐ Help shut down a plant, region, country product line, service, operation that has been around a reasonable amount of time.

☐ Work on a multi-functional team trying to solve an issue that crosses boundaries in the organization.

☐ Relaunch an existing product/service that's not doing well.

☐ Work on a team managing a significant business crisis (e.g., product scare, scandal, natural disaster, violent crime against employees, competitor significantly erodes market position).

☐ Manage a group where they are more expert in the technology than you are.

Striving for excellence motivates you;
striving for perfection is demoralizing.
Harriet Braiker – U. S. clinical psychologist

Suggested Readings

Antony, M. M., & Swinson, R. P. (2009). *When perfect isn't good enough: Strategies for coping with perfectionism* (2nd ed.). Oakland, CA: New Harbinger Publications, Inc.

Bardwick, J. M. (2002). *Seeking the calm in the storm: Managing chaos in your business life.* Upper Saddle River, NJ: Financial Times/Prentice Hall.

Calzada, L. (2007). *180 Ways to effectively deal with change: Get over it! Get with it! Get to it!* Flower Mound, TX: The Walk the Talk Company.

De Bono, E. (1999). *Six thinking hats* (2nd ed.). Boston, MA: Little, Brown and Co.

Gurvis, J., & Calarco, A. (2007). *Adaptability: Responding effectively to change.* Greensboro, NC: Center for Creative Leadership.

Handy, C. (1989). *The age of unreason.* Boston, MA: Harvard Business School Press.

Handy, C. (1994). *The age of paradox.* Boston, MA: Harvard Business School Press.

Kennedy, P. M. (1987). *The rise and fall of the great powers: Economic change and military conflict from 1500 to 2000.* New York, NY: Random House.

Nadler, G., & Hibino, S. (1998). *Breakthrough thinking: The seven principles of creative problem solving* (2nd ed.). Roseville, CA: Prima Publishing.

The Systems Thinker®. http://www.thesystemsthinker.com.

Weick, K. E., & Sutcliffe, K. M. (2007). *Managing the unexpected: Resilient performance in an age of uncertainty* (2nd ed.). San Francisco, CA: Jossey-Bass.

Wilkinson, D. (2006). *The ambiguity advantage: What great leaders are great at.* Hampshire, England: Palgrave Macmillan.

Wind, J., Crook, C., & Gunther, R. (2004). *The power of impossible thinking: Transform the business of your life and the life of your business.* Upper Saddle River, NJ: Wharton School Publishing.

Dimension 6
Essence

All truths are easy to understand once they are discovered;
the point is to discover them.
Galileo Galilei – Italian philosopher, astronomer, and mathematician

Skilled

Looks for root causes; interested in why; good at separating the more important from the less important.

Unskilled

May be too caught up in single events or problems and fail to see the pattern; may focus too narrowly on solutions based on present conditions; may view most things as about equally important and not differentiate well among different activities. At the extreme, could be an action junkie.

Items

- ☐ 6. Prefers to get to the root causes of things.
- ☐ 33. Likes finding the essence of why things work and don't work.
- ☐ 60. Looks for the why and how of events and experiences more than the what; searches for meaning.

Leadership Architect® Competencies Most Associated with This Dimension

Strong

- ☐ 2. *Dealing with* Ambiguity
- ☐ 46. Perspective
- ☐ 51. Problem Solving

Moderate

- ☐ 32. Learning on the Fly
- ☐ 50. Priority Setting
- ☐ 52. Process Management

Light

- ☐ 17. Decision Quality
- ☐ 41. Patience
- ☐ 43. Perseverance

33

6

Some Causes

☐ Complexifier
☐ Doesn't get to the point
☐ Doesn't go deep
☐ High need for speed
☐ High need to close
☐ Impatient
☐ Narrow background
☐ Not challenged
☐ Not curious
☐ Not strategic
☐ Satisfied with a temporary fix

Developmental Difficulty

Easier

The Map

Looking to patterns of how and why something works is what produces a robust solution. Simply looking at what has worked can be misleading as it may have only worked in certain conditions that no longer apply. To solve problems better, we need to understand patterns and causes. If you can get to the essence, then you can propose and implement the simplest and most elegant solution.

Some Remedies and Workarounds

☐ **1. Trouble differentiating? Start categorizing.** See how many causes for things you can come up with and how many categories you can put them in. Then ask what they have in common and how they are different.

☐ **2. Missing the point? Check for common errors in thinking.** Do you state as facts things that are really opinions or assumptions? Do your feelings or emotions get in the way of issues? Do you attribute cause and effect to relationships when you don't know if one causes the other? Do you generalize from a single example? Do you treat all aspects of a problem as if they are equally important?

☐ **3. Not detecting patterns? Study successes and ask what they have in common.** If you can find three times that something worked, ask why it worked despite differences in the situations. Also ask what was present in a failure that was never present in a success. Then you are on the way to finding principles that may repeat.

☐ **4. Rushing through problems? Take time to think.** Add a few minutes to your thinking time, go through a mental checklist without jumping at the first option. Since defining a problem and taking action tend to occur simultaneously, spend more time up front.

☐ **5. Skimming the surface? Start digging.** Locate the essence of a problem by figuring out its key elements. Experts usually figure out problems by locating the deep underlying principles and working forward from there. The less adept focus on desired outcomes/solutions and either work backward or focus on surface facts.

☐ **6. Stumped? Broaden your search for solutions.** Hunt for parallels in other organizations and in remote areas totally outside your field. By this we don't mean best practices, which come and go. Find a parallel situation to the underlying issue—for example, who has to do things really fast (Domino's, FedEx)? Who has to deal with maximum ambiguity (emergency room, a newspaper, police dispatchers)?

☐ **7. Overcomplicating things? Reach for Ockham's Razor.** Throughout the history of thought, the proposition has been put forward that the solution with the least number of elements or factors is probably the most correct one. See how few reasons you can create that explain the issue.

☐ **8. Impatient? Follow the key stages of problem solving.** There is a progression of getting to the essence of a problem or issue. Generally, problem solving starts with simplistic solutions to complex problems. First, everyone proposes a solution, even before there is a clear definition of the problem. The second stage is complexification. Someone always blows the issue out into its ultimate completeness with boxes and arrows. Many times it is correct, but very involved and complex. The third stage is parsimony. Someone takes all of the complexity and trims it down into the understandable. Some accuracy is lost. The last stage is simplicity or essence. Someone trims to the ultimate foundation-rock basis of the issue with an elegant and simple explanation or solution. One problem is that the simplistic and the simple look alike, although one is incorrect and the other accurate. The trick is to take the problem though the four stages. That takes patience. You can't get to the essence until you understand the complex.

☐ **9. *(Workaround)* Not motivated to dig for meaning? Leverage others' skills.** Engage internal or external essence detectors—people who enjoy and are good at getting to the very bottom of things. Give them everything you know and let them work at it for a while and report back. Ask them to walk you through their process for reaching the conclusions they have drawn.

☐ **10.** *(Workaround)* Don't want to start from scratch? Find out the history. In a sense, there are no new problems. Almost all problems have a history. It may be a new problem to you but probably not to the world. Look to history. See what people have done in the past. What did everyone decide, well after the fact, were the real causes and the real solutions?

More Help?

In addition to the 10 tips listed for this dimension, there are some tips that may apply from *FYI For Your Improvement*™. We have coded each item to about 10 tips from the *FYI* book. To use this resource, the codes below refer to the chapter and then the tip number from the *FYI* book. For example, in item 6 below, 17-3 refers to Chapter 17 – Decision Quality, tip 3. If you don't have a copy of *FYI*, it is available through Lominger International at 952-345-3610 or www.lominger.com.

6. Prefers to get to the root causes of things.

   17-3; 30-2,6; 32-1,2,3,10; 41-7; 51-1; 101-3

33. Likes finding the essence of why things work and don't work.

   17-3; 30-2,6; 32-1,2,3,10; 41-7; 51-1; 101-3

60. Looks for the why and how of events and experiences more than the what; searches for meaning.

   17-3; 30-2,6; 32-1,2,3,10; 41-7; 51-1; 101-3

Jobs That Would Add Skills in This Dimension

☐ Fix-Its/Turnarounds – requiring identifying the essential elements that cause the failure and the essential elements that will fix it.

☐ Heavy Strategic Demands – finding the essence of a new direction.

☐ International Assignments – where you have to identify the essential things to do and the essential differences from what you have known and done in the past.

☐ Staff Leadership (influencing without authority) – finding solutions to tough problems with insufficient direct power to make anything happen. The politics of the job are usually sensitive and opposition is common.

Part-Time Assignments That Would Add Skills in This Dimension

☐ Work with a highly diverse team to accomplish a difficult task.

☐ Work on a team fixing something that has failed.

☐ Take on a tough and undoable project where others have failed.

6

☐ Work on a team that has to integrate diverse systems (move from using five computer platforms into one), processes (integrating a distinct, stand-alone, quality-assurance process into a product development process), or procedures (five competency models into one) across decentralized and/or dispersed units where you have to boil things down to their essence.

☐ Relaunch an existing product/service that's not doing well.

☐ Work on a multi-functional team trying to solve an issue that crosses boundaries in the organization.

☐ Plan a new site for a building or installation (plant, field office, headquarters, etc.).

☐ Handle a tough negotiation with an external or internal customer, a union, a key vendor, or a dissatisfied customer.

☐ Work on a team managing a significant business crisis (e.g., product scare, scandal, natural disaster, violent crime against employees, competitor significantly erodes market position).

☐ Work on a team deciding whom to lay off and what to shut down to trim costs.

The truth is incontrovertible, malice may attack it,
ignorance may deride it, but in the end, there it is.
Winston Churchill – Former British Prime Minister,
orator, historian, Nobel Prize-winning writer, and artist

6

Suggested Readings

Andersen, B., & Fagerhaug, T. (2006). *Root cause analysis: Simplified tools and techniques* (2nd ed.). Milwaukee, WI: ASQ Quality Press.

Bazerman, M. H., & Moore, D. A. (2008). *Judgment in managerial decision making* (7th ed.). Hoboken, NJ: John Wiley & Sons.

De Bono, E. (1999). *Six thinking hats* (2nd ed.). Boston, MA: Little, Brown and Co.

Facione, P. A., & Facione, N. C. (2007). *Thinking and reasoning in human decision making: The method of argument and heuristic analysis.* Millbrae, CA: The California Academic Press.

Finkelstein, S., Whitehead, J., & Campbell, A. (2009). *Think again: Why good leaders make bad decisions and how to keep it from happening to you.* Boston, MA: Harvard Business School Press.

Gigerenzer, G. (2007). *Gut feelings: The intelligence of the unconscious.* New York, NY: Penguin Group.

Gladwell, M. (2007). *Blink: The power of thinking without thinking.* New York, NY: Little, Brown and Co.

Handy, C. (1994). *The age of paradox.* Boston, MA: Harvard Business School Press.

Latino, R. J., & Latino, K. (2006). *Root cause analysis: Improving performance for bottom-line results* (3rd ed.). Boca Raton, FL: CRC Press.

Paul, R. W., & Elder, L. (2002). *Critical thinking: Tools for taking charge of your professional and personal life.* Upper Saddle River, NJ: Financial Times/Prentice Hall.

The Systems Thinker®. http://www.thesystemsthinker.com.

Dimension 7
Inquisitive

The greatest virtue of man is perhaps curiosity.
Anatole France – French poet, journalist, novelist,
and winner of the Nobel Prize for Literature

Skilled
Searches for the new; curious, likes to have many things going at once.

Unskilled
Likes the familiar; may prefer to work on one thing at a time, go to comfortable sources, or be with comfortable people who won't challenge present conceptions.

Items
- ☐ 7. Is on the hunt for something new; seems to need fresh challenges.
- ☐ 34. Is more fascinated, amused, or intrigued with tough problems and challenges than stressed, troubled, or strained.
- ☐ 61. Is a curious person; is intellectually adventuresome.

Leadership Architect® Competencies Most Associated with This Dimension

Strong
- ☐ 2. *Dealing with* Ambiguity
- ☐ 14. Creativity

Moderate
- ☐ 32. Learning on the Fly
- ☐ 46. Perspective
- ☐ 51. Problem Solving

Light
- ☐ 1. Action Oriented
- ☐ 28. Innovation Management
- ☐ 61. Technical Learning

Some Causes

- ☐ Can't get out of the box
- ☐ Can't shift gears quickly
- ☐ Comfortable with what is
- ☐ Conventional
- ☐ Fear of uncertainty
- ☐ Gets frustrated easily
- ☐ Has a need to finish things before moving on
- ☐ Impatient
- ☐ Intimidated by things and people who are different
- ☐ Narrow background
- ☐ Not challenged
- ☐ Not curious
- ☐ Not wanting to be the only one out front
- ☐ Perfectionist

Developmental Difficulty

Moderate

The Map

Most of us fall into habitual ways of thinking and acting, and this in turn leads to diminishing our creativity and problem-solving skills. Learning about something new increases the chance of making novel connections. The curious always find the treasure.

Some Remedies and Workarounds

- ☐ 1. **Narrow background? Explore new ground.** Take a course in an area you know nothing about. Take a course in an area only sort of related to what you do. Go to restaurants you know nothing about. Vacation at places you've never been before. Talk to more strangers in line at the grocery store and on airplanes. Go to ethnic festivals. Watch several episodes of *Modern Marvels*, a cable program on the History Channel which answers the question "How did they do that?" You can buy the series.

- ☐ 2. **Playing it safe? Take more risks.** Research indicates that more successful people have made more mistakes than the less successful. You can't learn anything if you're not trying anything new. Start small and experiment a bit. Go for small wins so you can recover quickly if you miss and, more important, learn from the results. Start with the easiest challenge, then work up to the tougher ones.

□ **3. Bored or uncommitted? Create challenges.** Seen it all, done the same tasks again and again. Start with a list of what you like and don't like to do. Do at least a couple of liked activities each day, but follow a basic rule of psychology—least-preferred activities first. Reward yourself with the liked activities. Volunteer for task forces and projects that you would enjoy to modify your job. Don't focus on the activities you dislike—focus on what is accomplished and record them.

□ **4. Stuck in a rut? Get some fresh ideas.** Carve out some time and study something deeply, look for parallels outside your organization, find a good sounding board, talk to an expert in an unrelated field, talk to the most imaginative person you know, look for unusual facts that don't fit and ask what they might mean, use a storyboard to pictorially look at a problem or process.

□ **5. Old solutions not working? Use some new thinking tools.** Write down lists of pros and cons and then flowchart according to what's working and what isn't, run a scenario from A to Z, buy some planning software, look for the patterns in a problem rather than the solutions, convene a brainstorming session.

□ **6. Frustrated? Try a new approach.** Maybe you give up too soon. If you have trouble persisting beyond the first try, switch approaches. Think about multiple ways to get to the same outcome. For example, you could meet with stakeholders first, bring in an expert to make the case, meet with a single key person to get feedback, or call a problem-solving session and have the answer evolve from the discussion.

□ **7. Too wrapped up in today? Start looking ahead.** Don't like to speculate? Start reading international publications like the *Economist* and write down emerging trends. Research on the Internet topics that might affect your organization—see what leading thinkers are saying about them. Set a goal of coming up with three to five emerging trends.

□ **8. Small comfort zone? Go against the grain.** Fight sameness. Purposefully look outside the box. Look under the rocks for the new, different, and unique. Be outrageous and silly. Think like a child. Ask why again and again. Extend yourself. Be courageous and propose things at the margins.

□ **9. *(Workaround)* Not motivated to ask more questions? Leverage others' skills.** Engage internal or external resources who enjoy and are good at looking under rocks. Get creative people to look at it for you. Have them dig and find as many things as they can before you spend time on it.

7

☐ 10. *(Workaround)* Uncertain about your skills? Find a stand-in. Hire someone for your staff or team who is creative and innovative. Give them the tasks that require digging deep and looking for the new and different. Give them time and resources. Be patient. Always recognize their efforts whether you use what they come up with or not.

More Help?

In addition to the 10 tips listed for this dimension, there are some tips that may apply from *FYI For Your Improvement*™. We have coded each item to about 10 tips from the *FYI* book. To use this resource, the codes below refer to the chapter and then the tip number from the *FYI* book. For example, in item 7 below, 1-5,6 refers to Chapter 1 – Action Oriented, tips 5 and 6. If you don't have a copy of *FYI*, it is available through Lominger International at 952-345-3610 or www.lominger.com.

7. Is on the hunt for something new; seems to need fresh challenges.

1-5,6; 2-3; 6-3,4,6; 14-1; 43-1; 57-1; 118-8

34. Is more fascinated, amused, or intrigued with tough problems and challenges than stressed, troubled, or strained.

2-1,3; 14-1,2,9; 32-2,4; 51-1,4,8

61. Is a curious person; is intellectually adventuresome.

1-5; 14-1; 30-3,4; 32-9; 46-8,9; 51-1; 58-3; 118-8

Jobs That Would Add Skills in This Dimension

☐ Chair of Projects/Task Forces – where the issues might be new and first-time challenges, and those where you have to help others understand.

☐ Heavy Strategic Demands – finding the essence of a new direction.

☐ Line to Staff Switches – where you have to learn a new set of issues and problems in a new setting.

☐ Scope (complexity) Assignments – managing a high variety of activities at different levels of complexity and certainty.

☐ Start-Ups – requiring doing a lot of first-time things and meeting new challenges that need fixing in a short period of time.

Part-Time Assignments That Would Add Skills in This Dimension

☐ Work on a team fixing something that has failed.

☐ Work with a highly diverse team to accomplish a difficult task.

☐ Take on a tough and undoable project where others have failed.

☐ Relaunch an existing product/service that's not doing well.

☐ Launch a new product, service, or process.

□ Handle a tough negotiation with an external or internal customer, a union, a key vendor, or a dissatisfied customer.

□ Work on a team managing a significant business crisis (e.g., product scare, scandal, natural disaster, violent crime against employees, competitor significantly erodes market position).

□ Work on a multi-functional team trying to solve an issue that crosses boundaries in the organization.

□ Plan a new site for a building or installation (plant, field office, headquarters, etc.).

□ Work on a team that has to integrate diverse systems (move from using five computer platforms into one), processes (integrating a distinct, stand-alone, quality-assurance process into a product development process), or procedures (five competency models into one) across decentralized and/or dispersed units where you have to find the most common solution.

> *Intellectual growth should commence at birth*
> *and cease only at death.*
> Albert Einstein – German-born American physicist
> and Nobel Prize winner

7

Suggested Readings

Bolles, R. N. (2008). *What color is your parachute? 2009: A practical manual for job-hunters and career-changers.* Berkeley, CA: Ten Speed Press.

Cummings, I. (2008). *The vigorous mind: Cross-train your brain to break through mental, emotional, and professional boundaries.* Deerfield Beach, FL: Health Communications, Inc.

De Bono, E. (1999). *Six thinking hats* (2nd ed.). Boston, MA: Little, Brown and Co.

Freund, P. (2007). *A passion for discovery.* Hackensack, NJ: World Scientific Publishing Co.

Gigerenzer, G. (2007). *Gut feelings: The intelligence of the unconscious.* New York, NY: Penguin Group.

Marquardt, M. J. (2005). *Leading with questions: How leaders find the right solutions by knowing what to ask.* San Francisco, CA: Jossey-Bass.

Martin, R. (2007). *The opposable mind: How successful leaders win through integrative thinking.* Boston, MA: Harvard Business School Press.

Meyers, H. M., & Gerstman, R. (2007). *Creativity: Unconventional wisdom from 20 accomplished minds.* New York, NY: Palgrave Macmillan.

Root-Bernstein, M. M., & Root-Bernstein, R. S. (2001). *Sparks of genius: The thirteen tools of the world's most creative people.* New York, NY: Mariner Books.

Silvia, P. J. (2006). *Exploring the psychology of interest.* New York, NY: Oxford University Press, Inc.

Sternberg, R. J. (2007). *Wisdom, intelligence, and creativity synthesized.* New York, NY: Cambridge University Press.

New York Times. (2007). *The New York Times guide to essential knowledge: A desk reference for the curious mind* (2nd ed.). New York, NY: St. Martin's Press.

Dimension 8
Solution Finder

Every great and deep difficulty bears in itself its own solution.
It forces us to change our thinking in order to find it.
Niels Bohr – Danish physicist and winner of the Nobel Prize in Physics

Skilled
Ingenious problem solver; can combine parts of ideas, come up with missing pieces, play with different combinations, etc.

Unskilled
May have one way or too lockstep a method of problem solving; may be unwilling to play with the puzzle before him/her.

Items
- ☐ 8. Can combine the best parts of more than one idea or solution from multiple people and sources into a net better idea or solution.
- ☐ 35. Comes up with what's missing and can fill in the missing pieces as a method of getting information and solving problems.
- ☐ 62. Can play or fiddle with ideas to solve problems.

Leadership Architect® Competencies Most Associated with This Dimension

Strong
- ☐ 2. *Dealing with* Ambiguity
- ☐ 14. Creativity
- ☐ 46. Perspective
- ☐ 51. Problem Solving

Moderate
- ☐ 32. Learning on the Fly
- ☐ 52. Process Management

Light
- ☐ 33. Listening
- ☐ 40. *Dealing with* Paradox
- ☐ 41. Patience

Some Causes

- ☐ Conventional
- ☐ Doesn't dig deep enough
- ☐ Doesn't take the time
- ☐ Fear of uncertainty
- ☐ Impatient
- ☐ Lacks curiosity
- ☐ Narrow background
- ☐ Not creative
- ☐ Not experimental
- ☐ Perfectionist
- ☐ Relies on the past
- ☐ Stops too soon
- ☐ Wants to get things done in a hurry

Developmental Difficulty

Moderate

The Map

It's easy to fall into the habit of relying on our personal history. Have you seen a promising experiment abandoned because no one tried a new method to find a solution? Did each person simply reach into his or her standard bag of solutions and pull out a tired, timeworn approach? Unique, new, and different solutions fuel progress. To reach the new, the truly unique, takes some time. It takes hard work. It takes skill.

Some Remedies and Workarounds

- ☐ **1. Stuck in a rut? Get some fresh ideas.** Carve out some time and study something deeply, look for parallels outside your organization, find a good sounding board, talk to an expert in an unrelated field, talk to the most imaginative person you know, look for unusual facts that don't fit and ask what they might mean, use a storyboard to pictorially look at a problem or process.

- ☐ **2. Old solutions not working? Use some new thinking tools.** Write down lists of pros and cons and then flowchart according to what's working and what isn't, run a scenario from A to Z, buy some planning software, look for the patterns in a problem rather than the solutions, convene a brainstorming session.

- ☐ **3. Missing critical information? Ask more questions.** In one study of problem solving, 7% of comments were questions and about half were solutions. Others have shown that defining the problem and taking

46

action occur almost simultaneously, so the more effort you put up front, the better. Stop and define what the problem is and isn't, what causes it, and how many organizing buckets you can put the causes in. This increases the chance of a better solution because you can see more possible connections among problem elements.

☐ **4. Quick to take action? Don't go for the first solution.** Studies show on average that either the second or the third solution generated is usually superior.

☐ **5. Missing the point? Check for common errors in thinking.** Do you state as facts things that are really opinions or assumptions? Do your feelings or emotions get in the way of issues? Do you attribute cause and effect to relationships when you don't know if one causes the other? Do you generalize from a single example? Do you treat factors as if they are equally important?

☐ **6. Only seeing things one way? Flip your perspective.** Think in opposite cases when confronted with a tough problem. Turn the problem upside down. Ask what is the least likely thing the problem could be; what the problem is and is not; what's missing from the problem that, if there, would lead to a solution; or what the mirror image of the problem is.

☐ **7. Keep following the same path? Try out some oddball tactics.** What is a direct analogy between something you are working on and something in nature? Engineers once solved an overheating problem by drawing a parallel to what animal trainers do to calm upset or angry animals.

☐ **8. *(Workaround)* Looking for inspiration? Read biographies of famous people who had to come up with critical solutions.** Churchill, for example, always slept on an issue, no matter how urgent. Initially, he only asked questions to try to understand the issue. He kept his views to himself. See what you can learn from people you admire. A helpful Web site for finding biographical summaries, books, videos, etc. is www.biography.com. Additionally, they list a monthly schedule for the Biography Channel, a cable channel on the A&E Network dedicated to biography programs and specials on significant lives.

☐ **9. *(Workaround)* Not motivated to search for new solutions? Leverage others' talents.** Engage internal or external resources who enjoy and are good at coming up with creative, unique, different, and ingenious solutions to things. Let them work on it before you engage yourself.

☐ **10. *(Workaround)* Don't want to start from scratch? Look to history for solutions.** There are few really new problems. Look for parallel or similar situations. Log the solutions from the past. Test them out against the current issue.

More Help?

In addition to the 10 tips listed for this dimension, there are some tips that may apply from *FYI For Your Improvement*™. We have coded each item to about 10 tips from the *FYI* book. To use this resource, the codes below refer to the chapter and then the tip number from the *FYI* book. For example, in item 8 below, 14-2,3,4 refers to Chapter 14 – Creativity, tips 2,3, and 4. If you don't have a copy of *FYI*, it is available through Lominger International at 952-345-3610 or www.lominger.com.

8. Can combine the best parts of more than one idea or solution from multiple people and sources into a net better idea or solution.

   14-2,3,4; 17-3,5; 30-2; 32-2,3; 41-7; 101-3

35. Comes up with what's missing and can fill in the missing pieces as a method of getting information and solving problems.

   14-2,3,4; 17-3,5; 30-2; 32-2,3,6; 101-3

62. Can play or fiddle with ideas to solve problems.

   14-2,3,4; 17-3,5; 30-2; 32-2,3,6; 101-2

Jobs That Would Add Skills in This Dimension

☐ Heavy Strategic Demands – finding strategic solutions for tough marketplace challenges.

☐ International Assignments – where you are mostly on your own to find new or different solutions to tough problems in a setting that is different from your background.

☐ Scope (complexity) Assignments – managing a high variety of activities at different levels of complexity and uncertainty with lots of problems to find solutions for.

☐ Staff Leadership (influencing without authority) – finding solutions to tough, politically sensitive problems with insufficient direct power to make anything happen.

☐ Start-Ups – requiring finding solutions to first-time problems where there are no direct rules of thumb or reference points.

Part-Time Assignments That Would Add Skills in This Dimension

☐ Work with a highly diverse team to accomplish a difficult task.

☐ Take on a tough and undoable project where others have failed to find the solution.

☐ Work on a team moving a group through an unpopular change.

☐ Work on a team fixing something that has failed.

☐ Relaunch an existing product/service that's not doing well.

☐ Work on a multi-functional team trying to solve an issue that crosses boundaries in the organization.

☐ Manage a dissatisfied internal or external customer; troubleshoot a performance or quality problem with a new product or service.

☐ Work on a team managing a significant business crisis (e.g., product scare, scandal, natural disaster, violent crime against employees, competitor significantly erodes market position).

☐ Handle a tough negotiation with an external or internal customer, a union, a key vendor, or a dissatisfied customer.

☐ Plan a new site for a building or installation (plant, field office, headquarters, etc.).

Effective leadership is not about making speeches or being liked; leadership is defined by results not attributes.
Peter F. Drucker – U. S. writer and management consultant

FACTOR I: MENTAL AGILITY

8

Suggested Readings

Adair, J. (2009). *The art of creative thinking: How to be innovative and develop great ideas.* Philadelphia: Kogan Page.

De Bono, E. (1999). *Six thinking hats* (2nd ed.). Boston, MA: Little, Brown and Co.

Dettmer, H. W. (2007). *The logic thinking process: A systems approach to complex problem solving* (2nd ed.). Milwaukee, WI: American Society for Quality, Quality Press.

Hicks, M. J. (2004). *Problem solving and decision making: Hard, soft, and creative approaches* (2nd ed.). London: Thomson Learning.

Higgins, J. M. (2005). *101 Creative problem solving techniques: The handbook of new ideas for business* (Rev. ed.). Winter Park, FL: New Management Pub. Co.

Kahane, A., & Senge, P. M. (2007). *Solving tough problems: An open way of thinking, listening, and creating new realities* (2nd ed.). San Francisco, CA: Berrett-Koehler Publishers.

Kennedy, P. M. (1987). *The rise and fall of the great powers: Economic change and military conflict from 1500 to 2000.* New York, NY: Random House.

Michalko, M. (2006). *Thinkertoys: A handbook of creative thinking techniques* (2nd ed.). Berkeley, CA: Ten Speed Press.

Proctor, T. (2005). *Creative problem solving for managers: Developing skills for decision making and innovation* (2nd ed.). New York, NY: Routledge.

Roam, D. (2008). *The back of the napkin: Solving problems and selling ideas with pictures.* New York, NY: Penguin Group.

The Systems Thinker®. http://www.thesystemsthinker.com.

Von Oech, R. (2008). *A whack on the side of the head: How you can be more creative* (Rev. ed.). Dublin: Business Plus.

Watanabe, K. (2009). *Problem solving 101: A simple book for smart people.* New York, NY: Penguin Group.

Factor II
People Agility

High
This Factor measures self-management in relationship to others. In one sense, it is related to the concept of EQ (Emotional Quotient) or EI (Emotional Intelligence). People high on this Factor know themselves better and are more open-minded toward others. They seek feedback and respond to it through personal change. In interactions with others, they are seen as helpful, constructive even in disagreement, and open to diversity of people and viewpoints. They are clear in presenting viewpoints to others and are good at explaining their thinking and that of others. They relate to others well.

Low
People low on this Factor may not deploy themselves as well because they don't know themselves well: They over- or underestimate themselves and their skills, don't know their limits, or might mishandle situations that they think are being handled well. Lacking insight into self, they may lack it into others as well. Perhaps due to this, they might not handle conflict well, misreading or mishandling the situation. Leading change efforts may be a shortcoming due to some combination of inflexibility, lack of clear, calm transactions with others, political missteps, or not being seen as constructive with others.

Some Causes
- [ ] Doesn't care about others
- [ ] Doesn't listen
- [ ] Gets frustrated and has a temper
- [ ] Gets stressed or overwhelmed easily
- [ ] Impatient
- [ ] Misogynist or racist
- [ ] Narrow perspective
- [ ] Not in a feedback-rich situation
- [ ] Not observant
- [ ] Overly serious
- [ ] Resists feedback
- [ ] Self-centered
- [ ] Stuck in the past; prefers old ways
- [ ] Uncomfortable with face-to-face conflict
- [ ] Withdrawn or shy

Dimension 9
Agile Communicator

Think like a wise man but communicate in the language of the people.
William Butler Yeats – Irish poet and dramatist

Skilled
Considers the audience; is articulate, can make the complex understandable; uses appropriate language to sell a view; fairly presents the arguments of others.

Unskilled
May be inarticulate, appeal to an audience incorrectly, or be unable to present a complex argument; may overwhelm the audience with emotion or detail; may not characterize the arguments of others well.

Items
- ☐ 9. Can present ideas and concepts in the language of the target audience.
- ☐ 36. Can articulately explain complex ideas and concepts to others.
- ☐ 63. Is able to state opposing opinions and arguments clearly and without bias.

Leadership Architect® Competencies Most Associated with This Dimension

Strong
- ☐ 49. Presentation Skills
- ☐ 56. Sizing Up People
- ☐ 64. Understanding Others

Moderate
- ☐ 27. Informing
- ☐ 33. Listening
- ☐ 45. Personal Learning
- ☐ 51. Problem Solving

Light

☐ 12. Conflict Management
☐ 40. *Dealing with* Paradox
☐ 41. Patience
☐ 46. Perspective
☐ 47. Planning

Some Causes

☐ Can't simplify
☐ Doesn't handle conflict calmly
☐ Doesn't listen
☐ Doesn't read people or audiences well
☐ Goes too fast for others to keep up
☐ Impatient
☐ Inflexible and rigid
☐ Intolerant of slower people
☐ Not good integrating technology for presentations
☐ Not humorous
☐ Not planful
☐ Not quick on the uptake
☐ Shoots from the hip

Developmental Difficulty

Harder

The Map

It's all in the communicating. Nothing is more of a lubricant than that. You have to be able to convey meaning. You have to be able to tell others what you know. You have to be able to adjust your pace, style, and message to the audience. Knowing it yourself is seldom enough. Conveying is success.

Some Remedies and Workarounds

☐ **1. Unsure where to start? Focus on the main message**. State your message or purpose in a single sentence, then outline your talk around three to five things that support this thesis and that you want people to remember. Consider what an audience member should say 15 minutes after you finish.

☐ **2. Prone to lecture? Stick to key information.** Don't try to tell the audience all you know, even if they are well-informed on the topic. You are giving a persuasive argument or communicating key information; it's not a lecture. Drowning people in detail will lose even the most knowledgeable and interested.

☐ **3. Need to rehearse? Practice out loud.** Writing out a pitch or argument isn't useful until you say it. Writing sounds stilted when spoken because the cadence of speech and sentence length is generally quite different.

☐ **4. Overcomplicate the message? Watch out for jargon if you have to explain something complex.** Again, it's not a lecture. If you are speaking on a technical issue to a non-technical audience, present as if you were talking to a bright twelve-year-old. You're sure he or she will understand if you use straightforward language and logic.

☐ **5. One-trick pony? Vary your presentation by audience.** Some common questions to consider are: What's their time tolerance? How much do they expect to participate? Do they prefer formal or informal? Would they rather just chat about the topic? How sophisticated is the group? How much pushback do you expect?

☐ **6. Not speaking their language? Communicate in the language of the audience.** If you're a marketing person speaking with engineers, learn their conceptual categories by asking them how they would analyze it and what questions they would ask.

☐ **7. Talking head? Make your presentations more interactive.** Minimize your presentation and maximize two-way exchange with the audience. Present your points in outline format and encourage maximum discussion and dialogue.

☐ **8. Tell and sell? Listen and understand others' positions.** Make sure you know the points of view of others. Don't just tell and sell. Be able to clearly state their views.

☐ **9. *(Workaround)* Need an expert? Use a skilled presenter.** For critical presentations, engage someone who is a proven communicator to present your message for you. You provide the input and the key points. You might also introduce the speaker and set the stage for the audience.

☐ **10. *(Workaround)* Don't need to present in person? Use a recorded message.** Have someone video you delivering your message. Pilot it with someone you trust. Then, have someone else manage the event and present the pre-recorded message.

9

More Help?

In addition to the 10 tips listed for this dimension, there are some tips that may apply from *FYI For Your Improvement*™. We have coded each item to about 10 tips from the *FYI* book. To use this resource, the codes below refer to the chapter and then the tip number from the *FYI* book. For example, in item 9 below, 49-1,2,3,4,5 refers to Chapter 49 – Presentation Skills, tips 1,2,3,4 and 5. If you don't have a copy of *FYI*, it is available through Lominger International at 952-345-3610 or www.lominger.com.

9. Can present ideas and concepts in the language of the target audience.

    49-1,2,3,4,5; 64-8; 65-1,5; 67-3,4

36. Can articulately explain complex ideas and concepts to others.

    2-5; 27-6; 32-1,2,3; 49-2; 51-1,5; 52-3; 65-1

63. Is able to state opposing opinions and arguments clearly and without bias.

    12-1,2,3,4,5; 31-2; 33-7,8,9; 41-7

Jobs That Would Add Skills in This Dimension

☐ Cross-Moves – requiring communicating with a new group of people from another function.

☐ International Assignments – requiring communicating to a new and diverse population.

☐ Line to Staff Switches – requiring communicating with a new group of people with different functional homes and a different viewpoint on the world.

☐ Scope (complexity) Assignments – requiring communicating to a variety of people about a variety of topics.

☐ Significant People Demands – requiring communicating to a large number of people, usually in dispersed structures.

☐ Staff Leadership (influencing without authority) – communicating across organizational boundaries without the power to command attention.

☐ Start-Ups – requiring forging a new team and communicating on a variety of new and first-time subjects on a tight timetable.

Part-Time Assignments That Would Add Skills in This Dimension

☐ Work on a team moving a balky and resisting group through an unpopular change or project.

☐ Build a multi-functional team to tackle an issue that crosses boundaries in the organization.

☐ Work on a team that has to integrate diverse systems (move from using five computer platforms into one), processes (integrating a distinct, stand-alone, quality-assurance process into a product development process), or procedures (five competency models into one) across decentralized and/or dispersed units where you have to find the most common solution.

☐ Work with a highly diverse team to accomplish a difficult task.

☐ Work on a team fixing something that has failed.

☐ Relaunch an existing product/service that's not doing well.

☐ Handle a tough negotiation with an external or internal customer, a union, a key vendor, or a dissatisfied customer.

☐ Manage a renovation project.

☐ Represent the concerns of one group to another where the groups are substantially different (clerical and senior management, union and non-union, one country to another).

☐ Be a change agent; create symbols for change; lead the way; champion a significant change.

Everyone hears only what he understands.
Johann Wolfgang von Goethe – German playwright and novelist

Suggested Readings

Baldoni, J. (2003). *Great communication secrets of great leaders.* New York, NY: McGraw-Hill.

Brady, M. (2003). *Wisdom of listening.* Somerville, MA: Wisdom Publications.

Condrill, J., & Bough, B. (2005). *101 Ways to improve your communication skills instantly* (4th ed.). San Antonio, TX: GoalMinds, Inc.

Hoope, M. H. (2007). *Active listening: Improve your ability to listen and lead.* Greensboro, NC: Center for Creative Leadership.

Koegel, T. J. (2007). *The exceptional presenter: A proven formula to open up and own the room.* Austin, TX: Greenleaf Book Group Press.

Leeds, D. (2009). *PowerSpeak: Engage, inspire, and stimulate your audience* (Rev. ed.). Franklin Lakes, NJ: Career Press.

McKay, M., Davis, M., & Fanning, P. (2009). *Messages: The communication skills book* (3rd ed.). Oakland, CA: New Harbinger Publications.

Monarth, H., & Kase, L. (2007). *The confident speaker: Beat your nerves and communicate at your best in any situation.* New York, NY: McGraw-Hill.

Perkins, P. S., & Brown, L. (2008). *The art and science of communication: Tools for effective communication in the workplace.* Hoboken, NJ: John Wiley & Sons.

Presentations Magazine. www.presentations.com.

Siddons, S. (2008). *The complete presentation skills handbook: How to understand and reach your audience for maximum impact and success.* Philadelphia, PA: Kogan Page.

Weissman, J. (2006). *Presenting to win: The art of telling your story.* New York, NY: Prentice Hall.

Dimension 10
Conflict Manager

You can't shake hands with a clenched fist.
Indira Gandhi – Former Prime Minister of India

Skilled
Constructive with others; knows how to handle conflicts and disagreements; watches others closely and adjusts.

Unskilled
May have problems dealing with conflict or seeing and explaining others' points of view; may not gauge impact on others well.

Items
- ☐ 10. Even though he/she may not agree, understands and can explain the arguments and positions of others.
- ☐ 37. Can deal constructively with people he/she disagrees with, doesn't like, or is in conflict with on other issues.
- ☐ 64. Monitors others closely to gauge his/her impact and adjusts accordingly.

Leadership Architect® Competencies Most Associated with This Dimension
Strong
- ☐ 12. Conflict Management
- ☐ 33. Listening
- ☐ 56. Sizing Up People

Moderate
- ☐ 40. *Dealing with* Paradox
- ☐ 45. Personal Learning
- ☐ 51. Problem Solving
- ☐ 64. Understanding Others

Light

- ☐ 11. Composure
- ☐ 31. Interpersonal Savvy
- ☐ 32. Learning on the Fly
- ☐ 41. Patience
- ☐ 46. Perspective

Some Causes

- ☐ Avoids conflict
- ☐ Defensive
- ☐ Doesn't listen
- ☐ Gets stressed and frustrated easily
- ☐ Has strong viewpoints on everything
- ☐ Holds grudges
- ☐ Impatient
- ☐ Inflexible or rigid
- ☐ Not observant
- ☐ Not open to personal diversity
- ☐ Opinionated
- ☐ Self-centered
- ☐ Strong need to dominate
- ☐ Wants to win at all costs

Developmental Difficulty

Harder

The Map

A recent survey revealed that managers spend 18% of their time dealing with face-to-face conflict. Most organizations are decentralized and compartmentalized, which sets up natural conflict. Added to this is the accelerated pace of change where processes and procedures undergo near-constant tweaking. Dealing with and resolving conflict is of increasing importance. There is nothing more certain than uncertainty and the conflict that comes from it.

Some Remedies and Workarounds

☐ 1. **Have to win every battle? Give in order to get.** Some of us cause unnecessary conflict with our language and attitude toward winning. Do you challenge others and offer solutions and opinions too early? Increase the perception of fairness by focusing on common-ground issues. Try to find wins for both sides. Give in on little points. Avoid starting with strong positions. Give reasons first and solutions last.

☐ 2. **Do disagreements easily get out of hand? Keep conflicts small.** Find out what the points of agreement are rather than focusing on the disagreements only. Don't resort to general statements such as "We have trust problems with your unit." Keep the concern specific—stick to the specific whats and whens.

☐ 3. **Lose your cool? Keep emotions in check.** Sometimes our emotional reactions lead others to believe we can't handle conflict. Learn your telltale signs (raising your volume, drumming your fingers, shifting in your chair, etc.) and substitute something more useful. Pause, take a deep breath, ask a question, rephrase something until you can respond appropriately. Stay away from the personal. Stick to facts and problems; stay away from personalizing the issue.

☐ 4. **Only interested in your side of the story? Follow the rule of equity.** Explain your thinking and ask others to explain theirs. Be able to state their opinions as clearly as they can. Generate a variety of possibilities rather than staking out a rigid position. Keep your voice calm and speak briefly. Practice asking more questions and making fewer statements.

☐ 5. **Biased? Turn off the judgment switch.** Don't signal that you don't like someone or that they are wasting your time. Your goal should be to help and understand, not judge. Help others structure their arguments or be more concise. Focus on the strengths they have, not inevitable human shortcomings. Give second chances. Put your mind in neutral and ask questions.

☐ 6. **Impatient? Slow down.** Impatient people provide solutions too early in the process. Take time to really define the problem and hear people out. Figure out what questions need to be answered in order to resolve it.

☐ 7. **Unsure of others' reactions? Monitor the reactions of people to what you are doing or saying.** If they're bored, change the pace. Confused? State your argument differently. Angry? Stop and find out what's going on. Too quiet? Ask a question; get them engaged. Disinterested? Figure out what's in it for them. Be ready to adjust.

☐ **8. Feel like you're being attacked? Let the other side vent.** Listen. Nod. Ask clarifying questions. Ask open-ended questions like "What could I do to help?" Restate their position so they know you've heard them. You don't have to do anything to appease; just listen and accept that they are irritated. Your goal is to calm the situation so you can get back to more reasonable discussion.

☐ **9.** *(Workaround)* **Need outside help? Engage an internal or external resource who can help with conflict resolution.** Have him/her visit with the parties involved and summarize the nature of the conflict. Have him/her also suggest a number of methods for resolving as much of the conflict as possible.

☐ **10.** *(Workaround)* **Want to be more conflict-ready? Scan for potential conflicts.** Use someone close to you (possibly on your staff) to alert you to upcoming conflicts. You might also have them suggest optional strategies to defuse the conflict before it escalates. Practice upcoming conflicts in your mind. Run through a number of possible scenarios.

More Help?

In addition to the 10 tips listed for this dimension, there are some tips that may apply from *FYI For Your Improvement*™. We have coded each item to about 10 tips from the *FYI* book. To use this resource, the codes below refer to the chapter and then the tip number from the *FYI* book. For example, in item 10 below, 12-1,2,3,4,5 refers to Chapter 12 – Conflict Management, tips 1,2,3,4 and 5. If you don't have a copy of *FYI*, it is available through Lominger International at 952-345-3610 or www.lominger.com.

10. Even though he/she may not agree, understands and can explain the arguments and positions of others.

   12-1,2,3,4,5; 31-2; 33-7,8,9; 41-7

37. Can deal constructively with people he/she disagrees with, doesn't like, or is in conflict with on other issues.

   12-1,5,7; 33-7,9; 37-1,2; 41-7; 101-5; 104-4

64. Monitors others closely to gauge his/her impact and adjusts accordingly.

   31-2,3; 45-1,2,3,4,5,6,7; 104-4

Jobs That Would Add Skills in This Dimension

☐ Cross-Moves – requiring working with a new group of people from another function with a different background and viewpoint.

☐ Fix-Its/Turnarounds – requiring making tough decisions impacting a variety of people and constituencies.

10

☐ International Assignments – requiring conflicting cultures and a new and diverse population.

☐ Line to Staff Switches – requiring working with a new group of people with different functional homes and a different viewpoint on the world.

☐ Staff Leadership (influencing without authority) – communicating across organizational boundaries without the power to command attention where people and political skills are at a premium.

Part-Time Assignments That Would Add Skills in This Dimension

☐ Make peace with an enemy or someone you've disappointed or someone you've had some trouble with or don't get along with.

☐ Work on moving a balky and resisting group through an unpopular change or project.

☐ Help shut down a facility or office or territory and work on whom to keep and whom to let go.

☐ Handle a tough negotiation with an external or internal customer, a union, a key vendor, or a dissatisfied customer.

☐ Manage a dissatisfied internal or external customer; troubleshoot a performance or quality problem with a new product or service.

☐ Take on a tough and undoable project where others have failed before you and lots of other people are involved.

☐ Work on a team fixing something that has failed.

☐ Work with a highly diverse team to accomplish a difficult task.

☐ Work on a team that has to integrate diverse systems (move from using five computer platforms into one), processes (integrating a distinct, stand-alone, quality-assurance process into a product development process), or procedures (five competency models into one) across decentralized and/or dispersed units where you have to find the most common solution.

☐ Resolve a long-standing issue between groups where the groups are substantially different (clerical and senior management, union and non-union, one country to another).

Peace is not absence of conflict. It is the ability to handle conflict by peaceful means.
Ronald Reagan – 40th President of the United States

Suggested Readings

Blackard, K., & Gibson, J. W. (2002). *Capitalizing on conflict: Strategies and practices for turning conflict to synergy in organizations.* Palo Alto, CA: Davies-Black Publishing.

Cartwright, T. (2003). *Managing conflict with peers.* Greensboro, NC: Center for Creative Leadership.

Crawley, J., & Graham, K. (2002). *Mediation for managers: Getting beyond conflict to performance.* Yarmouth, ME: Nicholas Brealey Publishing.

Furlong, G. T. (2005). *The conflict resolution toolbox: Models and maps for analyzing, diagnosing, and resolving conflict.* Mississauga, ON: John Wiley & Sons Canada Ltd.

Gerzon, M. (2006). *Leading through conflict: How successful leaders transform differences into opportunities.* Boston, MA: Harvard Business School Press.

Harper, G. (2004). *The joy of conflict resolution: Transforming victims, villains, and heroes in the workplace and at home.* Gabriola Island, BC: New Society Publishers.

Jones, T. S., & Brinkert, R. (2007). *Conflict coaching: Conflict management strategies and skills for the individual.* Thousand Oaks, CA: Sage Publications.

Masters, M. F., & Albright, R. R. (2002). *The complete guide to conflict resolution in the workplace.* New York, NY: AMACOM.

Patterson, K., Grenny, J., McMillan, R., & Switzler, A. (2005). *Crucial confrontations: Tools for talking about broken promises, violated expectations, and bad behavior.* New York, NY: McGraw-Hill.

Perlow, L. (2003). *When you say yes but mean no: How silencing conflict wrecks relationships and companies...and what you can do about it.* New York, NY: Crown Business.

Popejoy, B., & McManigle, B. J. (2002). *Managing conflict with direct reports.* Greensboro, NC: Center for Creative Leadership.

Runde, C. E., & Flanagan, T. A. (2006). *Becoming a conflict competent leader: How you and your organization can manage conflict effectively.* San Francisco, CA: Jossey-Bass.

Dimension 11
Cool Transactor

That is the happiest conversation where there is no competition, no vanity,
but a calm, quiet interchange of sentiments.
Samuel Johnson – English poet, essayist, and novelist

Skilled
Unbiased; can easily state cases he or she disagrees with like an accomplished debater; accurate, fair, others will listen to what this person says.

Unskilled
May be alternately too passionate and one-sided or a poor listener/articulator of others' notions; at the extreme, may be viewed as overly self-sufficient and uncaring.

Items
- ☐ 11. Uses objective and adjective-free language even when he/she feels strongly about things so as to not chill interactions.
- ☐ 38. Is good at delivering even negative feedback to others; can get others to listen.
- ☐ 65. Is politically adept; knows how to work with key decision makers and stakeholders.

Leadership Architect® Competencies Most Associated with This Dimension

Strong
- ☐ 11. Composure
- ☐ 12. Conflict Management
- ☐ 56. Sizing Up People
- ☐ 64. Understanding Others

Moderate
- ☐ 31. Interpersonal Savvy
- ☐ 36. Motivating Others
- ☐ 41. Patience

Light

☐   2. *Dealing with* Ambiguity
☐   8. Comfort Around Higher Management
☐ 13. Confronting Direct Reports
☐ 33. Listening
☐ 34. Managerial Courage

Some Causes

☐ Avoids conflict
☐ Defensive
☐ Dislikes politics
☐ Doesn't listen
☐ Easily stressed or frustrated
☐ Holds grudges
☐ Impatient
☐ Inflexible
☐ Insensitive to others
☐ Intolerant of differences
☐ Opinionated
☐ Too personally involved

Developmental Difficulty

Harder

The Map

Turning down the volume and depersonalizing tough transactions are key aspects of persuasion and problem solving. Noise seldom helps. The brain turns down when the heat is turned up.

Some Remedies and Workarounds

☐ 1. **Difficulty staying on point? Go from specific to general points.** Keep to the facts. Don't embellish and don't say everything you know or feel. If feelings are involved, wait until you can describe them, not show them.

☐ 2. **Dance around negative feedback? Get to the point.** Don't waste time with a long preamble when the feedback is negative. If the recipient is likely to know what's coming, go ahead and say it directly. They won't hear anything positive until later anyway. If you have to be critical, you can still empathize with how he/she feels, and you can help with encouragement when the discussion turns more positive. Mentally rehearse these worst-case scenarios.

☐ **3. Does your word choice fuel the fire? Tone down your language.** Do you blame with inflammatory words? Do your words become impersonal and sterile? Either approach will blow the transaction for you. Speak to the person in a way you would like to be treated in the same situation. Avoid condescending terms like "What you need to understand" or "This is the third time...." Both imply the receiver is either stupid or unwilling. Keep your volume in the mid-range. Avoid any critical or negative humor. While this may make you feel better, it will cut like a knife.

☐ **4. Use sweeping statements? Keep all discussion specific.** Don't generalize. Don't use loaded words like "trust" or anything that impugns intelligence or suggests ill motives. Don't pick words that are personal, blaming, or autocratic. Be more tentative and probabilistic: "Might it be that" or "What seems to have occurred here is this." Use language that invites dialogue.

☐ **5. Poor speaking habits? Improve your vocabulary and delivery.** Avoid using the same words repeatedly, using filler words like "uh" and "you know," speaking too rapidly or forcefully, or going into so much detail that people can't follow the point. Outline arguments. Know the three things you're trying to say and say them succinctly. Others can always ask questions if something is unclear.

☐ **6. Need to barter? Vary your style according to group and objectives.** Work from the outside in. Determine the demands of the situation and select what style will play with a particular person or group. Think of any discussion as a quid pro quo. If you ask for help, what help can you provide in return. If people see you as competitive, they will cut you out of the loop. Establish common ground. Give in order to get.

☐ **7. Unclear where others stand on an issue? Listen more.** Do you really know how others see the issue or do you tell and sell? Do you even know if it is important to them? Don't interrupt. Don't suggest words or solutions when they pause. Don't cut them off by saying, "I already know that," "I've heard that before," or the dreaded "But that won't work." Help them say what they need to say.

☐ **8. Lack knowledge about different groups? Be an anthropologist.** Learn what a group believes and why they believe it. What are their hot buttons? What's their goal? Nothing will kill you quicker with a group than to show utter disregard for their norms and views. Do your homework. If that's not possible, listen and ask lots of questions.

☐ **9. Tend to rush in to confront issues? Establish a waiting period.** Rehearse what you need to say until you can say it without inflammatory or blameful language. Don't get caught having to deliver your message on the spur of the moment. Be planful. Pick your spots.

☐ 10. *(Workaround)* **Trouble delivering bad news in person? Engage an internal or external person to deliver the message.** Sometimes an HR professional might be used to pass on some corrective information you can't calmly handle. Or arrange a situation where the person will get the same message through some other method like a 360° or a course with feedback.

More Help?

In addition to the 10 tips listed for this dimension, there are some tips that may apply from *FYI For Your Improvement*™. We have coded each item to about 10 tips from the *FYI* book. To use this resource, the codes below refer to the chapter and then the tip number from the *FYI* book. For example, in item 11 below, 11-1,2,7,8 refers to Chapter 11 – Composure, tips 1,2,7 and 8. If you don't have a copy of *FYI*, it is available through Lominger International at 952-345-3610 or www.lominger.com.

11. Uses objective and adjective-free language even when he/she feels strongly about things so as to not chill interactions.
    11-1,2,7,8; 12-2,5,7; 27-6; 41-1,2

38. Is good at delivering even negative feedback to others; can get others to listen.
    12-3,5,7; 31-3,6; 34-1,3,4,10; 45-1

65. Is politically adept; knows how to work with key decision makers and stakeholders.
    48-2,3,5,7; 64-5,6,8; 119-1,4,5

Jobs That Would Add Skills in This Dimension

☐ Crisis Manager or Change Manager – requiring tough-minded decisions under tight time pressure with a low level of consultation.

☐ Fix-Its/Turnarounds – requiring making tough decisions impacting a variety of people and constituencies.

☐ Significant People Demands – requiring a high volume of people decisions and transactions, many times without much consultation.

☐ Staff Leadership (influencing without authority) – working across organizational boundaries without the power to command attention where people and political skills are at a premium; conflict cannot be resolved with authority; influence is the main tool.

☐ Start-Ups – rapid decisions need to be made without much consultation.

Part-Time Assignments That Would Add Skills in This Dimension

☐ Work on moving a balky and resisting group through an unpopular change or project.

☐ Work on a team fixing something that has failed.

☐ Help shut down a facility or office or territory and work on whom to keep and whom to let go.

☐ Manage the outplacement of a number of people.

☐ Handle a tough negotiation with an external or internal customer, a union, a key vendor, or a dissatisfied customer.

☐ Manage a dissatisfied internal or external customer; troubleshoot a performance or quality problem with a new product or service.

☐ Manage the assigning/allocation of office space in a contested situation where everyone can't win or be satisfied.

☐ Resolve a long-standing issue between groups where the groups are substantially different (clerical and senior management, union and non-union, one country to another).

☐ Be a change agent; create symbols for change; lead the way; champion a significant change.

☐ Take on a tough and undoable project where others have failed before you and lots of other people are involved.

The pursuit, even of the best things, ought to be calm and tranquil.
Marcus Tullius Cicero (106 BCE - 43 BCE)
– Ancient Roman philosopher, writer, and scholar

FACTOR II: PEOPLE AGILITY

11

Suggested Readings

Bolton, R. (1986). *People skills: How to assert yourself, listen to others and resolve conflicts.* New York, NY: Simon & Schuster, Inc.

Bradberry, T., & Greaves, J. (2005). *The emotional intelligence quick book: Everything you need to know to put your EQ to work.* New York, NY: Fireside.

Brady, M. (2003). *Wisdom of listening.* Somerville, MA: Wisdom Publications.

Brinkman, R., & Kirschner, R. (2002). *Dealing with people you can't stand* (Rev. ed.). New York, NY: McGraw-Hill.

Carter, L. (2003). *The anger trap: Free yourself from the frustrations that sabotage your life.* New York, NY: John Wiley & Sons.

Ferris, G. R., Davidson, S. L., & Perrewe, P. L. (2005). *Political skill at work: Impact on work effectiveness.* Mountain View, CA: Davies-Black Publishing.

Lerner, H. (2002). *The dance of connection: How to talk to someone when you're mad, hurt, scared, frustrated, insulted, betrayed, or desperate.* New York, NY: Quill/HarperCollins.

McIntyre, M. G. (2005). *Secrets to winning at office politics: How to achieve your goals and increase your influence at work.* New York, NY: St. Martin's Press.

Newman, J. (2007). *How to stay cool, calm, and collected when the pressure's on.* New York, NY: AMACOM.

Patterson, K., Grenny, J., McMillan, R., & Switzler, A. (2002). *Crucial conversations: Tools for talking when stakes are high.* New York, NY: McGraw-Hill.

Shepard, G. (2005). *How to manage problem employees: A step-by-step guide for turning difficult employees into high performers.* Hoboken, NJ: John Wiley & Sons.

Weitzel, S. R. (2007). *Feedback that works: How to build and deliver your message.* Greensboro, NC: Center for Creative Leadership.

Dimension 12
Helps Others Succeed

It is literally true that you can succeed best and quickest by helping others to succeed.
Napoleon Hill – American author

Skilled
Likes to see others do well; generous in credit and help.

Unskilled
May be too self-sufficient or uncaring; may envy the successes of others, fearing competition or being shown up; may see success as a zero-sum game.

Items
- ☐ 12. Brings out the best in others; lets others shine and finds something they can contribute.
- ☐ 39. Is more a credit giver and sharer than a taker.
- ☐ 66. Generally likes others to succeed regardless of his/her personal evaluation or opinion of them.

Leadership Architect® Competencies Most Associated with This Dimension

Strong
- ☐ 18. Delegation
- ☐ 27. Informing
- ☐ 36. Motivating Others

Moderate
- ☐ 20. Directing Others
- ☐ 23. Fairness to Direct Reports
- ☐ 41. Patience

Light
- ☐ 19. Developing Direct Reports and Others
- ☐ 33. Listening
- ☐ 40. *Dealing with* Paradox
- ☐ 56. Sizing Up People
- ☐ 60. *Building Effective* Teams

71

Some Causes

- ☐ A loner
- ☐ Doesn't take the time
- ☐ Doesn't understand people
- ☐ Excessively high standards
- ☐ Fear of failure
- ☐ Grandstander
- ☐ Insensitive
- ☐ Impatient
- ☐ Jealous of others
- ☐ Judgmental
- ☐ Selfish
- ☐ Short-term perspective
- ☐ Too competitive
- ☐ Unappreciative

Developmental Difficulty

Easier

The Map

Helping others, including your boss, succeed helps you succeed. There is a limited amount any of us can accomplish, regardless of how hard we work. Everyone knows this, but delegation and developing others are extremely weak skills in most organizations. Quite often we don't know how to help others succeed.

Some Remedies and Workarounds

- ☐ 1. **Won't risk giving out critical work? Get comfortable handing over control to others.** Why aren't you delegating? Are you a perfectionist, wanting everything to be just so? Unrealistic expectations? If this is you, expect career trouble. Better managers delegate more than managers who try to control most things. The keys are setting priorities, providing help, and designing workflows, not your personal effort.

- ☐ 2. **Unsure how to delegate? Set clear expectations, then get out of the way.** Communicate, set time frames and goals. Be very clear on what and when, be very open on how. People are more motivated when they can determine the how themselves. Encourage them to try things. Delegate complete tasks, not pieces. Allow more time than it would take you to do it.

- ☐ 3. **Accustomed to giving the answers? Be a teacher.** Always explain your thinking. Work out loud with them on a task. What do you see as important? How do you know? What questions are you asking? What steps are you following? Simply firing out solutions will make people more dependent at best.

☐ **4. Want your people to grow? Learn how to develop others.** Developing direct reports and others is dead last in skill level among the 67 Competencies of the Leadership Architect® and has been since we started collecting these data. To develop people, you have to follow the essential rules of development. They take a bit of time. Development is not simply sending someone to a course:

- Start with a portrait of the person's strengths and weaknesses. They can't grow if they are misinformed about themselves.
- Provide ongoing feedback from multiple sources.
- Give them progressively stretching tasks that are first-time and different for them. At least 70% of reported development occurs through challenging assignments that demand skill development. People don't grow from doing more of the same.
- Encourage them to think of themselves as learners, not just accomplishers. What are they learning that is new or different? What skills have improved in the last year? What have they learned that they can use in other situations?
- Use coursework, books, development partners, and mentoring to reinforce learning.

☐ **5. Not bringing out the best in people? Follow the basic rules of motivating others.** Communicate that what they do is important and how it's important. Offer help and ask for it. Provide autonomy and job challenge. Provide variety. Show an interest in their careers. Adopt a learning attitude toward mistakes. Celebrate successes. Set up reasonable goals that people can measure themselves against.

☐ **6. Playing favorites? Be equitable.** Don't use information as a reward for a few. Invite everyone's thinking, regardless of what you think of his or her level of performance. Turn off your judgment program and check to make sure you're not playing favorites or excusing behavior in a high performer that you wouldn't tolerate from anyone else. A neutral observer should not be able to tell from your demeanor who you favor and who you don't. Help the quiet, reserved and the shy have their say. Keep fairness conflicts small and concrete.

☐ **7. Always in the spotlight? Promote the careers of others.** Help others solve their problems, let others present and get the credit. Gain stature through the success of your people.

☐ **8.** *(Workaround)* **Looking for a systematic way to motivate? Use rewards and recognition programs.** Set up a more formal reward and recognition system that is reasonably automatic and doesn't require you to stop and think about it. Install objective standards of fairness (performance standards, pay, office choices, days off).

☐ **9.** *(Workaround)* **Want to empower your people? Have your team manage rewards and recognition with your input and guidance.** Let them decide on the standards and criteria and manage the selection process. Ask others around you for their opinions on who deserves rewards and recognition.

☐ **10.** *(Workaround)* **Recognition program too narrow in scope? Keep a reward and recognition log for both hard (money) and soft (a positive comment).** Try to balance the rewards among those you are responsible for, and try to hit everyone as often as you can.

More Help?

In addition to the 10 tips listed for this dimension, there are some tips that may apply from *FYI For Your Improvement*™. We have coded each item to about 10 tips from the *FYI* book. To use this resource, the codes below refer to the chapter and then the tip number from the *FYI* book. For example, in item 12 below, 18-1,5,8 refers to Chapter 18 – Delegation, tips 1, 5, and 8. If you don't have a copy of *FYI*, it is available through Lominger International at 952-345-3610 or www.lominger.com.

12. Brings out the best in others; lets others shine and finds something they can contribute.

18-1,5,8; 19-1,2,3,4,6; 36-3,10

39. Is more a credit giver and sharer than a taker.

18-1; 36-1; 103-3,8,9; 104-4,6,7,8,9

66. Generally likes others to succeed regardless of his/her personal evaluation or opinion of them.

23-2,3,4,5; 103-3,8,9; 104-4,8,9

Jobs That Would Add Skills in This Dimension

☐ Fix-Its/Turnarounds – requiring helping people rapidly change what they are doing and building their skills to be more successful.

☐ Scale (size shift) Assignments – managing larger numbers of people and being responsible for their current and future performance.

☐ Significant People Demands – requiring managing a large number of people, including responsibility for their training and development.

☐ Start-Ups – requiring forging a new team and building new skills as you go.

Part-Time Assignments That Would Add Skills in This Dimension

☐ Manage a group of green, novice, inexperienced, or new employees as their coach, teacher, mentor, or guide.

☐ Mange a group of people where you are the towering expert and they need to know what you do and be able to do what you do.

☐ Manage a group of low-competence people through a task they could not do by themselves.

☐ Work on moving a balky and resisting group through an unpopular change or project.

☐ Work on a team fixing something that has failed, where the same team who failed will stay to do it right.

☐ Work with a very diverse team of people to work on a tough issue none of them have done before, including you.

☐ Create employee involvement teams.

☐ Manage a group of people in a rapidly expanding unit that has to learn new things quickly.

☐ Build a multi-functional team to tackle an issue that crosses boundaries in the organization where no one person has all of the skills necessary to complete the task.

☐ Coach a sports team with new and inexperienced players (like youth soccer).

It is amazing what you can accomplish if you do not care who gets the credit.
Harry S. Truman – 33rd President of the United States

75

Suggested Readings

Dittmer, R. E., & McFarland, S. (2008). *151 Quick ideas for delegating and decision making*. Franklin Lakes, NJ: Career Press.

Ensher, E. A., & Murphy, S. E. (2005). *Power mentoring: How successful mentors and protégés get the most out of their relationships*. San Francisco, CA: Jossey-Bass.

Genett, D. M. (2004). *If you want it done right, you don't have to do it yourself! The power of effective delegation*. Sanger, CA: Quill/HarperCollins.

Harvard Business School Press. (2004). *Coaching and mentoring: How to develop top talent and achieve stronger performance*. Boston, MA: Harvard Business School Press.

Kirkpatrick, D. L. (2006). *Improving employee performance through appraisal and coaching* (2nd ed.). New York, NY: AMACOM.

Kouzes, J. M., & Posner, B. Z. (2003). *Encouraging the heart: A leader's guide to rewarding and recognizing others*. San Francisco, CA: Jossey-Bass.

Loehr, A., & Emerson, B. (2008). *A manager's guide to coaching: Simple and effective ways to get the best from your employees*. New York, NY: AMACOM.

Manzoni, J. F., & Barsoux, J. L. (2002). *The set-up-to-fail syndrome*. Boston, MA: Harvard Business School Press.

McBee, S. (2003). *To lead is to empower: Leadership to empower your employees and yourself*. New York, NY: Shar McBee.

12

Dimension 13
Light Touch

A well-developed sense of humor is the pole that adds
balance to your steps as you walk the tightrope of life.
William A. Ward – American author

Skilled
Uses humor well; knows how to lighten things up.

Unskilled
May be too serious or not use comic relief to relieve tension.

Items
- ☐ 13. Uses humor as a tool to get things done.
- ☐ 40. Can laugh at self.
- ☐ 67. Has fun at almost everything he/she does.

Leadership Architect® Competencies Most Associated with This Dimension

Strong
- ☐ 26. Humor
- ☐ 44. Personal Disclosure
- ☐ 45. Personal Learning

Moderate
- ☐ 11. Composure
- ☐ 12. Conflict Management
- ☐ 31. Interpersonal Savvy
- ☐ 46. Perspective
- ☐ 55. Self-Knowledge

Light
- ☐ 3. Approachability
- ☐ 36. Motivating Others
- ☐ 56. Sizing Up People
- ☐ 57. Standing Alone
- ☐ 64. Understanding Others

13

13

Some Causes
☐ Defensive and sensitive
☐ Doesn't see the humor in things
☐ Fear of being seen as silly
☐ Humorless
☐ Impatient
☐ Insensitive
☐ Low tolerance for diversity in style
☐ Low tolerance for uncertainty
☐ Overly serious
☐ Perfectionist
☐ Politically incorrect
☐ Shy or withdrawn
☐ Slow to catch on to humor
☐ Strong belief in separating personal from business
☐ Too planful and orderly
☐ Very private person

Developmental Difficulty
Harder

The Map
Humor and personal disclosure increase the involvement of others, make tough tasks seem more doable, relieve monotony, and contribute to a positive learning climate. Having a light touch can make a lot of things lighter for you and others.

Some Remedies and Workarounds
☐ 1. **Unsure what's funny? Find the fun in everyday events.** Whether you're naturally funny or not, it's easy to use humor. It's in the news, in jokes, kids and pets, universal human foibles, a ridiculous situation you've been caught in lately. It's a question of tuning into and using what is around you.

☐ 2. **Politically incorrect? Use humor sensibly.** Steer clear of political, ethnic, anything that makes fun of a whole group, and angry humor. Some people use humor to deliver sarcastic messages like "Oh, thanks for telling me that," or "I would have never thought of that." Sarcastic humor puts down the person in a way that is hard to recover from, essentially indicating the person is a dodo for saying this.

☐ 3. **Playing it safe? Laugh at yourself.** Self-humor is usually safe. Funny stories about when you were embarrassed or about your latest household project that resulted in five trips to the hardware store or calling in an expert. Personal goofs humanize us to others.

☐ 4. **Tight-lipped? Disclose more to others.** Good kinds of disclosure are the reasons behind how you do or think about something at work, tidbits of important information you can share without breaching confidences, commentary about what's going on without being too negative about others, and what is coming up that will affect them. All of these build relationships and assist in performance.

☐ 5. **Information scarcity? Beef up your messages.** Maybe you don't inform enough or are selective in informing. Informing is generally seen as an important skill that many people are not good at. When you see coworkers, ask yourself what you can share to help them do their jobs better.

☐ 6. **Looking to bring a light touch to your team? Build a sense of fun for those around you.** Parties, roasts, gag awards, and outings build cohesion. Start celebrating wins, honor those who have gone the extra mile, but don't honor anyone twice before everyone has been honored once. Working with the whole person tends to build teams.

☐ 7. **Need practice? Study up on it.** Read *How to Be Funny* by Jon Macks (New York: Simon & Schuster, 2003).

☐ 8. *(Workaround)* **Looking to infuse humor into presentations? Engage an internal or external speechwriter who is good at the lighter side.** Have him/her suggest places for humorous quotes and cartoons that would lighten up your communications.

☐ 9. *(Workaround)* **Not funny yourself? Delegate the fun planning to your staff.** Let them plan the light and the humorous. Cooperate as best you can. Put on your happiest face.

☐ 10. *(Workaround)* **Looking for visuals? Use humorous illustrations.** Display cartoons in your workspace and in your presentations. Use them to set a tone and give others something light to comment on to break the ice.

13

FACTOR II: PEOPLE AGILITY

13

More Help?

In addition to the 10 tips listed for this dimension, there are some tips that may apply from *FYI For Your Improvement*™. We have coded each item to about 10 tips from the *FYI* book. To use this resource, the codes below refer to the chapter and then the tip number from the *FYI* book. For example, in item 13 below, 26-1,2,3,4,5,6,7,8,9,10 refers to Chapter 26 – Humor, tips 1–10. If you don't have a copy of *FYI*, it is available through Lominger International at 952-345-3610 or www.lominger.com.

13. Uses humor as a tool to get things done.

   26-1,2,3,4,5,6,7,8,9,10

40. Can laugh at self.

   26-1,3,7,8,9; 44-1,2,5,6; 60-7

67. Has fun at almost everything he/she does.

   1-6; 26-1,3,8,9,10; 44-1,2; 60-7; 118-8

Jobs That Would Add Skills in This Dimension

☐ Jobs are not a significant source of skill building in this area.

Part-Time Assignments That Would Add Skills in This Dimension

☐ Help people write speeches with humor in them.

☐ Plan and run events (like off-sites) that have fun and silliness built into the activities.

☐ Be part of a team that puts on a humorous skit at a meeting.

☐ Volunteer to work for a charity or community organization to build your experiences with a broader spread of people.

☐ Work on a team that plans and carries out public relations activities or sales promotion events where some humor is present.

☐ Create and deliver a number of humorous stories about yourself at work and at play.

☐ Work on 10 self-humor statements or phrases you can use with people.

Humor distorts nothing, and only false gods are laughed off their earthly pedestals.
Agnes Repplier – American essayist

Suggested Readings

Adams, S. (1997). *The Dilbert Principle: A cubicle's-eye view of bosses, meetings, management fads, and other workplace afflictions.* New York, NY: HarperCollins.

Bradberry, T., & Greaves, J. (2005). *The emotional intelligence quick book: Everything you need to know to put your EQ to work.* New York, NY: Fireside.

Brinkman, R., & Kirschner, R. (2002). *Dealing with people you can't stand* (Rev. ed.). New York, NY: McGraw-Hill.

Carter, L. (2003). *The anger trap: Free yourself from the frustrations that sabotage your life.* New York, NY: John Wiley & Sons.

Davis, M., Eshelman, E. R., McKay, M., & Fanning, P. (2008). *The relaxation & stress reduction workbook* (6th ed.). Oakland, CA: New Harbinger Publications.

Hemsath, D., & Yerkes, L. (2001). *301 Ways to have fun at work.* San Francisco, CA: Berrett-Koehler Publishers.

Lerner, H. (2002). *The dance of connection: How to talk to someone when you're mad, hurt, scared, frustrated, insulted, betrayed, or desperate.* New York, NY: Quill/HarperCollins.

Losyk, B. (2004). *Get a grip! Overcoming stress and thriving in the workplace.* Hoboken, NJ: John Wiley & Sons.

Newman, J. (2007). *How to stay cool, calm, and collected when the pressure's on.* New York, NY: AMACOM.

Schwab, P. (2005). *Leave a mark, not a stain! What every manager needs to know about using humor in the workplace.* Seattle, WA: Rollingwood Press.

Willis, E. E., & Weaver, R. L. (2005). *How to be funny on purpose.* Toronto, ON: Cybercom.

13

13

Dimension 14
Open Minded

The open-minded see the truth in different things:
the narrow-minded see only the differences.
– Author Unknown

Skilled
Open to others, can change his/her mind; deals well with the differing actions and beliefs of others; open to new ideas, solutions.

Unskilled
Only or most comfortable with those most like him/her; not particularly open to different viewpoints; probably prefers tried-and-true solutions.

Items
- ☐ 14. Is tolerant of diversity in thought, actions, beliefs, and behaviors.
- ☐ 41. Is comfortable managing diversity in others.
- ☐ 68. Free from past solutions or the way things have usually been done; approaches current problems with an open mind.

Leadership Architect® Competencies Most Associated with This Dimension

Strong
- ☐ 2. *Dealing with* Ambiguity
- ☐ 46. Perspective

Moderate
- ☐ 21. *Managing* Diversity
- ☐ 32. Learning on the Fly
- ☐ 33. Listening
- ☐ 64. Understanding Others

Light
- ☐ 12. Conflict Management
- ☐ 14. Creativity
- ☐ 51. Problem Solving
- ☐ 56. Sizing Up People

Some Causes

- ☐ Doesn't listen
- ☐ Doesn't take the time
- ☐ Fear of the unknown
- ☐ High standards
- ☐ Impatient
- ☐ Inflexible or rigid
- ☐ Low tolerance of diversity
- ☐ Narrow background
- ☐ Not observant
- ☐ One best solution
- ☐ Opinionated
- ☐ Perfectionist
- ☐ Set in past ways
- ☐ Too conventional

Developmental Difficulty

Harder

The Map

Better learners collect more viewpoints and are more open to ideas and actions they don't necessarily agree with or want to do. The issue is what you can learn or gain from this, not what you personally care to do or believe. Open leads to more, closed leads to less.

Some Remedies and Workarounds

- ☐ 1. **Suffering from groupthink? Include varying viewpoints in discussions.** Heterogeneous or diverse groups are more innovative than homogeneous groups. The findings indicate that the more variety in the group, the fresher the ideas. Pick five people not like you (in specialty, level, gender/ ethnic group, background, history) and get to know how they think about the problems you face.

- ☐ 2. **Selectively open? Avoid putting people in buckets of those who can help you and those who can't.** Once you do that, the good bucket will get most of your attention. To break out of this, work on understanding without judging. Ask more questions, be a detective. You'll be pleasantly surprised at what you can gain from talking with people you don't ordinarily spend much effort on.

- ☐ 3. **One-sided interactions? Establish the rule of reciprocity.** Relationships don't last unless you provide something and you receive something in return. Find out what they want and tell them what you want. Learn how

14

they think, what their conceptual categories are, what key factors they look at, and what kinds of questions they ask. Pick something in their argument that you agree with and reinforce this. All of these expand your thinking.

☐ **4. Think you need to have all the answers? Avoid being a know-it-all.** Nothing says closed to others like solution-minded, seen-it-all-before behavior. By all means, lay out your thinking and explore alternatives, but don't make closing statements too early. You'll learn basically nothing from others.

☐ **5. Not approachable? Manage the first three minutes.** This is the key time to be open and approachable. Open, approachable people get more done. Talk later than you usually do. Take in information, feel people out, listen. Don't come on strong because you're busy. Some key tests for this:
  – Are you an early knower of information?
  – Do people give you lots of information and ideas?
  – Are people willing to do things for or with you?

☐ **6. Tempted to jump to solutions? Define the problem, not the solution.** Engage others in the whys, whats, and hows of what you are working on. Generate multiple solutions, don't settle on the first one. Be more aware of your biases. Do you drag out favorite solutions or reject anything that will force you to have to read a lot or interact with new people a lot? Go against your natural grain to be more open to different problem-solving techniques.

☐ **7. Accustomed to going it alone? Expand your network.** Use people as sounding boards, convene a one-time problem-solving group, or find a buddy group in another function or organization that faces a similar problem.

☐ **8. Quick to discount opinions that differ from yours? Try to think through or even present the viewpoints of the opposition.** How did they form those viewpoints? If you were in their shoes, would you have come to the same conclusion? What do they not know that prevented them from coming to your conclusion? What have you learned by coldly examining their viewpoints that might change yours?

☐ **9. *(Workaround)* Want to learn how others think? Use a formal exercise.** Systems like DeBono's Six Hats of Thinking (*Serious Creativity*, New York: HarperBusiness, 1993) can help guide you and your group through tough issues. Use the Myers-Briggs Type Indicator® to help you and your group understand how each person functions and processes information and to teach you and the group about diversity of style.

14

□ 10. *(Workaround)* Need to test your assumptions? Check your viewpoints with a disinterested person first before you disclose them. Find someone you trust who has no stake in the issue. Test out your viewpoint to check for bias.

More Help?

In addition to the 10 tips listed for this dimension, there are some tips that may apply from *FYI For Your Improvement*™. We have coded each item to about 10 tips from the *FYI* book. To use this resource, the codes below refer to the chapter and then the tip number from the *FYI* book. For example, in item 14 below, 21-6 refers to Chapter 21 – *Managing* Diversity, tip 6. If you don't have a copy of *FYI*, it is available through Lominger International at 952-345-3610 or www.lominger.com.

14. Is tolerant of diversity in thought, actions, beliefs, and behaviors.

　　21-6; 31-1,2,3,4; 64-6,8,9; 101-4; 104-4

41. Is comfortable managing diversity in others.

　　21-1,2,5,6,8; 23-2; 64-5,6; 101-4,5

68. Free from past solutions or the way things have usually been done; approaches current problems with an open mind.

　　14-1; 51-1,2,3,5,8; 101-2,3,4; 118-8

Jobs That Would Add Skills in This Dimension

□ Cross-Moves – requiring working with a new group of people from another function with a different background and viewpoint.

□ Fix-Its/Turnarounds – requiring helping people rapidly change what they are doing and building their skills to be more successful.

□ International Assignments – requiring conflicting cultures and a new and diverse population.

□ Significant People Demands – requiring managing a large number of people, including responsibility for their training and development.

Part-Time Assignments That Would Add Skills in This Dimension

□ Assemble a team of diverse people to accomplish a difficult task.

□ Integrate diverse systems, processes, or procedures across a decentralized or dispersed unit.

□ Form a multi-functional team to tackle a common issue.

□ Be a member of a union-negotiating or grievance-handling team.

□ Resolve a conflict between two people or two units.

□ Manage the renovation of an office, floor, building, warehouse, etc.

☐ Create and manage employee involvement teams.

☐ Handle customer complaints and suggestions.

☐ Manage a team of multi-nationals solving a common problem.

☐ Lobby for your organization on a contested issue in local, regional, state, federal, or international government.

There never were in the world two opinions alike, no more than two hairs or two grains; the most universal quality is diversity.
Michel de Eyquem Montaigne – French philosopher, writer, and statesman

14

FACTOR II: PEOPLE AGILITY

Suggested Readings

Ancona, D., Malone, T. W., Orlikowski, W. J., & Senge, P. M. (2007). In praise of the incomplete leader. *Harvard Business Review, 85*(2), 92-100.

Brady, M. (2003). *Wisdom of listening.* Somerville, MA: Wisdom Publications.

Donoghue, P. J., & Siegel, M. E. (2005). *Are you really listening? Keys to successful communication.* Notre Dame, IN: Sorin Books.

Finkelstein, S. (2003). *Why smart executives fail: And what you can learn from their mistakes.* New York, NY: Portfolio.

Goldsmith, M., & Reiter, M. (2007). *What got you here won't get you there: How successful people become even more successful.* New York, NY: Hyperion.

Harvey, C., & Allard, M. J. (2008). *Understanding and managing diversity* (4th ed.). Upper Saddle River, NJ: Prentice Hall.

Hoope, M. H. (2007). *Active listening: Improve your ability to listen and lead.* Greensboro, NC: Center for Creative Leadership.

Steger, U., Amann, W., & Maznevski, M. (Eds.). (2007). *Managing complexity in global organizations.* West Sussex, England: John Wiley & Sons.

Thiederman, S. (2008). *Making diversity work: Seven steps for defeating bias in the workplace.* New York, NY: Kaplan Business.

Thomas, R. J. (2008). *Crucibles of leadership: How to learn from experience to become a great leader.* Boston, MA: Harvard Business School Press.

Weick, K. E., & Sutcliffe, K. M. (2007). *Managing the unexpected: Resilient performance in an age of uncertainty* (2nd ed.). San Francisco, CA: Jossey-Bass.

Wilkinson, D. (2006). *The ambiguity advantage: What great leaders are great at.* Hampshire, England: Palgrave Macmillan.

14

Dimension 15
People Smart

Although I cannot lay an egg, I am a very good judge of omelettes.
George Bernard Shaw – Irish playwright, literary critic,
and Nobel Prize and Oscar winner

Skilled
Interested in what people have to say; pays attention; is good at sizing up people.

Unskilled
May misread others; may have trouble seeing their strengths and weaknesses clearly; people's views may not have much impact on him/her.

Items
- ☐ 15. Can empathize (put him/herself in the shoes of others).
- ☐ 42. Seems to get something out of interacting with others; works to gain from interactions.
- ☐ 69. Makes quick and mostly accurate judgments about people.

Leadership Architect® Competencies Most Associated with This Dimension
Strong
- ☐ 21. *Managing* Diversity
- ☐ 51. Problem Solving
- ☐ 56. Sizing Up People

Moderate
- ☐ 32. Learning on the Fly
- ☐ 33. Listening
- ☐ 64. Understanding Others

Light
- ☐ 2. *Dealing with* Ambiguity
- ☐ 36. Motivating Others
- ☐ 46. Perspective
- ☐ 55. Self-Knowledge

15

Some Causes

☐ Doesn't care about others
☐ Doesn't listen
☐ Doesn't take the time
☐ Excessively high standards
☐ Impatient
☐ Narrow people background
☐ No interest in people
☐ No need for people
☐ Not curious
☐ Not observant
☐ Sees people in too simple terms
☐ Self-centered
☐ Too critical
☐ Too quick to judge
☐ Uses stereotypes

Developmental Difficulty

Harder

The Map

A key skill at any level is figuring out what people's strengths and weaknesses are so you can gain from their strengths and either help them develop or learn to discount their views in their weak or flat areas. Predicting what people will do in certain situations makes you better able to adjust and respond. Knowing people well leads to selecting better people. Knowing what people can do makes you a better manager. There's no downside to being able to read people.

Some Remedies and Workarounds

☐ 1. **View people through a narrow lens? Avoid generalizing about others.** Just because someone is inept at their job doesn't mean they don't know how to do a hundred things better than you do. Just because someone is a star doesn't mean they don't have weaknesses.

☐ 2. **Drawn to those like yourself? Watch out for those you feel most comfortable with.** They are likely to be similar in personality, political views, and skill set. There's not as much you can learn from an echo of yourself. Seek out variety, people who grate on you or whom you often disagree with. Work on understanding what they do well and not well. Turn off your judgment program.

☐ **3. Difficulty opening up for others? Get to know people.** Hear people out, find out what drives people and what their career aspirations are. Find out what you have in common. Give in order to get. Share the same information about yourself.

☐ **4. Impatient? Follow the rules of listening.** Don't interrupt, don't finish sentences, don't wave off further input by saying you already know something. Ask more questions if you want to learn to size up people better.

☐ **5. Uncertain of how you are reading others? Challenge your assumptions.** See if you can write down three specific strengths and three specific weaknesses for everyone you work with closely, then decide how sure you are of this assessment. You will probably be quite sure for people who are more like you or whom you have a personal relationship with, and less sure for those more remote. Spend time with all the people on your list until you feel comfortable that you know three true strengths and three need areas for everyone.

☐ **6. Not sure what differences make a difference? Identify differentiating competencies.** There are five or more validated descriptions of work behaviors that are related to performance. Use the categories of experts, not your homegrown ones, to size up people. Test the model against people you have worked with closely across time (some you may no longer work with). See if you can differentiate the more talented from the less talented using this model. What strengths did both groups have in common? Which were different? What weaknesses did they share? Which were different? Use this to become less personal in your talent assessment. Most of us have characteristics we value (too much), downsides we excuse, and weaknesses we think are killers. Human competence is much more complex than our personal views. Learn to differentiate key competencies from the competencies that most people already have (basic intelligence, action orientation) and from the ones that are more likely to make a difference (such as sizing up people, dealing with ambiguity).

☐ **7. Not paying attention to what others say or do? Observe more.** See if you can predict what people are going to say and do before they do it. See if their behavior shows a pattern. See when they surprise you. By observing people more carefully, you get two benefits: You know their strengths and weaknesses better, and you can better adjust to their responses.

☐ 8. *(Workaround)* Expert people-reader available? Use an internal or external person who is a known accurate evaluator of people. Or poll a number of people you respect who tend to be more accurate than you are for their opinions before you settle into a viewpoint.

☐ 9. *(Workaround)* Looking for validation? Use formal assessments. Use assessment centers, 360° feedback, simulations, a psychologist, or testing to get a more formal opinion about others.

☐ 10. *(Workaround)* Need tools to assist in your evaluation? Use assisted assessment. Use a questionnaire, a sort card competency deck, a piece of software, or a set of structured questions to help you structure your assessments of key people around you.

More Help?

In addition to the 10 tips listed for this dimension, there are some tips that may apply from *FYI For Your Improvement*™. We have coded each item to about 10 tips from the *FYI* book. To use this resource, the codes below refer to the chapter and then the tip number from the *FYI* book. For example, in item 15 below, 7-1,2,3,4,5,6,8 refers to Chapter 7 – Caring about Direct Reports, tips 1,2,3,4,5,6 and 8. If you don't have a copy of *FYI*, it is available through Lominger International at 952-345-3610 or www.lominger.com.

15. Can empathize (put him/herself in the shoes of others).

7-1,2,3,4,5,6,8; 10-6,8,10

42. Seems to get something out of interacting with others; works to gain from interactions.

31-3,5,8,10; 33-3,6,9; 101-2,3,5

69. Makes quick and mostly accurate judgments about people.

33-4,5; 45-7; 56-1,3,4,6,7; 111-1,3

Jobs That Would Add Skills in This Dimension

☐ Cross-Moves – requiring working with a new group of people from another function with a different background and viewpoint.

☐ International Assignments – requiring conflicting cultures and a new and diverse population.

☐ Significant People Demands – requiring managing a large number of people, including responsibility for their training and development.

☐ Staff Leadership (influencing without authority) – working across organizational boundaries without the power to command attention where people and political skills are at a premium; conflict cannot be resolved with authority; influence is the main tool.

☐ Start-Ups – requiring forging a new team and building new skills as you go.

Part-Time Assignments That Would Add Skills in This Dimension

☐ Be a member of a union-negotiating or grievance-handling team.

☐ Assemble a team of diverse people to accomplish a difficult task.

☐ Help shut down a plant, office, product line, business, operation, etc.

☐ Resolve a conflict between two people or two units.

☐ Manage a team of multi-nationals solving a common problem.

☐ Handle a tough negotiation with an internal or external client or customer.

☐ Integrate diverse systems, processes, or procedures across a decentralized or dispersed unit.

☐ Train and work as an assessor in an assessment center.

☐ Represent to higher management the concerns of a group of non-exempt, clerical, administrative, or union employees to seek a resolution of a difficult issue.

☐ Be a member of the campus interviewing team.

☐ Do a study of highly successful managers and contrast that to managers who have failed in your organization, including interviewing people who know or knew them, and report your findings to top management.

Prejudice is opinion without judgment.
Voltaire – French philosopher and writer

Suggested Readings

Bradberry, T., & Greaves, J. (2005). *The emotional intelligence quick book: Everything you need to know to put your EQ to work.* New York, NY: Fireside.

Brislin, R. (2008). *Working with cultural differences: Dealing effectively with diversity in the workplace.* Santa Barbara, CA: Praeger Publishers.

Dimitrius, J., & Mazzarella, W. P. (2008). *Reading people: How to understand people and predict their behavior—anytime, anyplace.* New York, NY: Random House.

Dittmer, B., & McFarland, S. (2008). *151 Quick ideas to improve your people skills.* Franklin Lakes, NY: Career Press.

Goleman, D. (2006). *Emotional intelligence: Why it can matter more than IQ.* New York, NY: Bantam Books.

Goleman, D., Boyatzis, R., & McKee, A. (2004). *Primal leadership: Leaning to lead with emotional intelligence.* Boston, MA: Harvard Business School Press.

Goman, C. K. (2008). *The nonverbal advantage: Secrets and science of body language at work.* San Francisco, CA: Berrett-Koehler Publishers.

Klaus, P. (2007). *The hard truth about soft skills: Workplace lessons smart people wish they'd learned sooner.* New York, NY: Collins Business.

Peterson, B. (2004). *Cultural intelligence: A guide to working with people from other cultures.* Yarmouth, ME: Intercultural Press.

Segal, J. (2008). *The language of emotional intelligence: The five essential tools for building powerful and effective relationships.* New York, NY: McGraw-Hill.

Thomas, D. C., & Inkson, K. (2004). *Cultural intelligence: People skills for global business.* San Francisco, CA: Berrett-Koehler Publishers.

Dimension 16
Personal Learner

Leadership and learning are indispensable to each other.
John F. Kennedy – 35th President of the United States

Skilled
A continuous improver; actively seeks personal learning and skill building.

Unskilled
May be comfortable with current skills; at the extreme, may fear the missteps that go with growth or be afraid to tackle personal projects.

Items
- [ ] 16. Seeks and looks forward to opportunities for new learning experiences in business or personal areas.
- [ ] 43. Finds new things to learn and get good at.
- [ ] 70. Actively seeks out role models, living or dead, real or fictional, that can be helpful in learning or problem solving.

Leadership Architect® Competencies Most Associated with This Dimension

Strong
- [ ] 32. Learning on the Fly
- [ ] 45. Personal Learning
- [ ] 46. Perspective
- [ ] 54. Self-Development

Moderate
- [ ] 2. *Dealing with* Ambiguity
- [ ] 12. Conflict Management
- [ ] 51. Problem Solving

Light
- [ ] 33. Listening
- [ ] 55. Self-Knowledge
- [ ] 56. Sizing Up People

16

95

Some Causes

- ☐ Comfortable with what is
- ☐ Doesn't see consequences
- ☐ Doesn't take the time
- ☐ Fear of failure
- ☐ Given up
- ☐ Happy and satisfied
- ☐ Impatient
- ☐ Lack of ambition
- ☐ Lack of self-awareness
- ☐ Lazy
- ☐ Low risk taker
- ☐ Low standards of excellence
- ☐ Not curious
- ☐ Not inspired
- ☐ Rigid and inflexible
- ☐ Stuck in the past

Developmental Difficulty

Harder

The Map

Learning new skills is a prime predictor of promotion and career success. Being an eager learner has been related to everything from sales success to level attained in organizations. The world is bigger for active learners.

Some Remedies and Workarounds

- ☐ 1. Lost your passion for the job? Make a list of what you like to do and don't like to do. Concentrate on doing a few things you like each day. See if you can delegate or trade for more desirable activities. Do your least-preferred activities first. Focus not on the activity but on your sense of accomplishment. Volunteer for task forces and projects that would be more interesting for you.

- ☐ 2. Stuck in a rut? Get out of your comfort zone. Find an activity that goes against your natural likes and try it. Up your risk comfort. Start small so you can recover quickly. Pick a few smaller tasks or challenges and build the skill bit by bit. For example, if strategy is your area, write a strategic plan for your unit and show it to people to get feedback, then write a second draft. Devise a strategy for turning one of your hobbies (i.e., photography) into a business.

☐ 3. **Want to build on what you already know? Use your strengths to grow in new areas.** If you are planful, plan how you will attack a new area. If you are interpersonally smooth, imagine yourself using your contacts and your network to learn something new.

☐ 4. **Unsure of your current skill level? Learn your strengths and weaknesses.** Get a full 360° feedback from multiple sources and follow up with boss and Human Resources to see where you most need to improve.

☐ 5. **Not sending the message that you are a learner? Show others you take your development seriously.** State your development needs and ask for help. Research shows that people are much more likely to help and think favorably of those who admit their shortcomings.

☐ 6. **Need new learning techniques? Build a learning toolkit.** Many excellent learners have a grab bag of tactics. They ask lots of questions, save any solution statements for last, look outside their current line of work for parallels, keep a learning journal to capture insights, and so on.

☐ 7. **Narrow worldview? Be more adventuresome.** Travel to places you have not been before, go to ethnic festivals and talk to participants about their culture, scan the newspaper for events in your area you have never attended. Serve with a community group; volunteer.

☐ 8. **Is the company your learning lab? Pick three tasks you've never done before and go do them.** For example, if you don't know much about customers, work in a store or handle complaints; get placed on task forces that will require new learning for you.

☐ 9. **Looking for expert advice? Seek out role models.** Access great minds like John Stuart Mill on problem solving, or read a biography of Lyndon Johnson to learn about persuasion. Find three people who are excellent at something you want to develop in. Observe them, interview them, and see what they do that you do not. Ask them to think through an issue with you, what questions they would ask, and what they think good sources of knowledge are.

☐ 10. *(Workaround)* **Adapting to a role? Think of yourself as an actor.** An actor acts the part needed to make the play or movie work. Who they are is less important. Who they need to be is most important. Think about each key situation. How would Russell Crowe or Julia Roberts play the part? Body language? Voice? Pace? Process? Reactions? What are you trying to accomplish? What parts of you would work the best. See what works and what doesn't work.

16

FACTOR II: PEOPLE AGILITY

16

More Help?

In addition to the 10 tips listed for this dimension, there are some tips that may apply from *FYI For Your Improvement*™. We have coded each item to about 10 tips from the *FYI* book. To use this resource, the codes below refer to the chapter and then the tip number from the *FYI* book. For example, in item 16 below, 1-6 refers to Chapter 1 – Action Oriented, tip 6. If you don't have a copy of *FYI*, it is available through Lominger International at 952-345-3610 or www.lominger.com.

16. Seeks and looks forward to opportunities for new learning experiences in business or personal areas.

   1-6; 14-1; 32-4; 45-6,7,8; 54-1,10; 57-9; 118-8

43. Finds new things to learn and get good at.

   1-6; 46-1,5,7,8,9,10; 58-3; 61-7; 118-8

70. Actively seeks out role models, living or dead, real or fictional, that can be helpful in learning or problem solving.

   1-6; 6-2; 30-10; 32-5; 46-2,3,6,8; 103-5; 118-8

Jobs That Would Add Skills in This Dimension

☐ Cross-Moves – requiring working with a new group of people from another function with a different background and viewpoint.

☐ Heavy Strategic Demands – requiring significant strategic thinking and planning which charts new ground, along with selling it to a critical audience.

☐ International Assignments – requiring conflicting cultures and a new and diverse population.

☐ Scope (complexity) Assignments – requiring communicating to a variety of people about a variety of topics.

☐ Start-Ups – requiring forging a new team and building new skills as you go.

Part-Time Assignments That Would Add Skills in This Dimension

☐ Assemble a team of diverse people to accomplish a difficult task.

☐ Take on a tough and previously undoable project where others have tried but failed to come up with the right answer.

☐ Manage a group or a team of people who are towering experts in something you are not.

☐ Make peace with an enemy or someone you've disappointed with a product or service or someone you've had some trouble with or don't get along with very well.

☐ Teach a course, seminar, or workshop on something you don't know well.

☐ Attend a self-awareness workshop that has 360° and live feedback.

☐ Handle a tough negotiation with an internal or external client or customer.

☐ Integrate diverse systems, processes, or procedures across a decentralized or dispersed unit.

☐ Help shut down a plant, office, product line, business, operation, etc.

☐ Go on a business trip to a foreign country you've not been to before.

☐ Manage a team of multi-nationals solving a common problem.

> *The purpose of learning is growth, and our minds, unlike our bodies,*
> *can continue growing as long as we live.*
> Mortimer Adler – American philosopher and educator

16

Suggested Readings

Billett, S. (2008). *Learning in the workplace: Strategies for effective practice.* Crows Nest, Australia: Allen & Unwin Academic.

Finkelstein, S. (2003). *Why smart executives fail: And what you can learn from their mistakes.* New York, NY: Penguin Group.

Gladwell, M. (2008). *Outliers: The story of success.* New York, NY: Little, Brown and Co.

Goldsmith, M., & Reiter, M. (2007). *What got you here won't get you there: How successful people become even more successful.* New York, NY: Hyperion.

Merriam, S. B., Caffarella, R. S., & Baumgartner, L. M. (2006). *Learning in adulthood: A comprehensive guide.* San Francisco, CA: Jossey-Bass.

Pavlina, S. (2008). *Personal development for smart people: The conscious pursuit of personal growth.* Carlsbad, CA: Hay House.

Pedler, M., Burgoyne, J., & Boydell, T. (2007). *A manager's guide to self-development.* Berkshire, England: McGraw-Hill.

Thomas, R. J. (2008). *Crucibles of leadership: How to learn from experience to become a great leader.* Boston: MA: Harvard Business School Press.

16

Dimension 17
Responds to Feedback

*The only man who never makes a mistake
is the man who never does anything.*
Theodore Roosevelt – 26th President of the United States

Skilled
Comfortable with personal change, isn't paralyzed by mistakes; seeks feedback and moves on.

Unskilled
Closed, low interest in feedback or change; may deny or minimize mistakes and shortcomings. At the extreme, may be seen as self-important or, alternately, reticent.

Items
- ☐ 17. Seeks feedback.
- ☐ 44. Is insightful about personal mistakes and failures; learns from them and moves on.
- ☐ 71. Have seen this person substantially change based upon critical feedback, making a mistake, or learning something new.

Leadership Architect® Competencies Most Associated with This Dimension

Strong
- ☐ 45. Personal Learning
- ☐ 54. Self-Development

Moderate
- ☐ 12. Conflict Management
- ☐ 33. Listening
- ☐ 55. Self-Knowledge
- ☐ 56. Sizing Up People

Light
☐ 2. *Dealing with* Ambiguity
☐ 32. Learning on the Fly
☐ 44. Personal Disclosure
☐ 51. Problem Solving
☐ 57. Standing Alone

Some Causes
☐ Avoids conflict
☐ Avoids feedback
☐ Believes he/she's perfect
☐ Defensive
☐ Doesn't invite people in
☐ Doesn't listen
☐ Doesn't read others well
☐ Doesn't trust others
☐ Hard to approach
☐ Not ambitious
☐ Quick to blame others
☐ Rigid and inflexible
☐ Shy and withdrawn

Developmental Difficulty
Harder

The Map
Others view people who seek critical feedback more positively. People who seek positive feedback get the opposite response. The former shows willingness to improve. The latter is often seen as defensiveness and a disinterest in really knowing oneself. People who know themselves better do better. People who seek out feedback get more. Remember, whether you ask or not, everyone around has an opinion. Better to know.

Some Remedies and Workarounds
☐ 1. **Need all-around feedback? Get formal feedback with a 360°.** People who don't know their strengths and weaknesses tend to overestimate themselves, a consistent finding in the research literature that has been related to both poor performance and being terminated. 360° feedback, where you compare your responses on a set of competencies to those of boss, peers, direct reports (if any), and sometimes customers is the preferred approach. Many other avenues are open to you as well—boss, confidantes, or a development partner if you're lucky enough to have one.

□ 2. **Unsure how to get the most out of formal feedback? Focus on the highest and lowest ratings from each group.** Don't spend time worrying about whether your scores are high or low in an absolute sense. 360° instruments aren't designed as performance assessments ordinarily. For development, you should worry about you relative to you. What are your highest and lowest ratings?

□ 3. **Looking for root causes? Ask why.** Why am I seen this way? How did my strengths get to be so? Are my weaknesses things I avoid, things I'm simply not skilled at, things I dislike or things I've never done? What experiences shaped my pattern? Do I have strengths that are related to my weaknesses, such as the smart person who makes others feel less so? Use this analysis to determine what is relatively easier and tougher for you to do.

□ 4. **Some behaviors more troubling to you than others? Solicit written feedback.** Prepare specific areas you are concerned about and ask people to respond in writing. Ask them what they would like to see you keep doing, start doing, stop doing, or do differently. If you know the people well, you can try face-to-face feedback, although you should know that this is usually blander and more positive than written feedback. If you do this, select specific areas and state what you think the issue or need for improvement is. Don't ask general questions. Get them to respond to your statements.

□ 5. **Seen as arrogant and/or defensive? Be open to feedback.** Many people with a need in this area are seen as self-sufficient and disinterested in feedback and change. If this is the case, you may have to ask repeatedly. And regardless of the feedback, accept it. Don't say it's inaccurate or a one-time failing; don't argue or qualify. Just take it in. Use mental rehearsal to get ready for what may happen. If you comment at all, give examples of the behavior being described to validate what they are saying. Chances are good they are right. Defensive and arrogant people typically have major blind spots.

□ 6. **Has perception become reality? Show your true intent through action.** Even if the feedback is not true, you need to deal with it. If people, especially those above you, believe these things, your career will be damaged. You need to construct a plan to convince people of the untruth(s) by deeds, not words. Plan how you will act in critical situations, and expect it to take quite a while for people to see you differently. It may take 10 times before people reconsider their view of you.

□ 7. **Think expressing doubt shows weakness? Disclose more.** If you deny, minimize, or excuse away mistakes and shortcomings, take a chance and admit that you're imperfect like everyone else. Let your inside thoughts out in the open more often. Sprinkle normal work conversation with

17

doubts, what you're thinking about, and what's getting in the way. Since you probably don't know how to do this, select three people who are good at admitting mistakes and shortcomings and observe how they do it.

☐ **8. Afraid of mistakes? Take responsibility.** Admit mistakes matter-of-factly, inform everyone potentially affected, learn from it so the mistake isn't repeated, then move on. Dwelling on the past is useless. Build up your heat shield. Successful people make lots of mistakes. Being right much more than two-thirds of the time is impossible if you're doing anything new. Don't let the possibility of being wrong keep you from standing up and trying.

☐ **9. (Workaround) Uncertain where to begin? Start by becoming more self-aware.** Just make it a goal to know yourself completely without worrying about doing anything about your weaknesses. Ask everyone you respect. Do a 360° feedback assessment. Research has shown that just knowing about all of your weaknesses can actually lead to some improvement without actually working on them.

☐ **10. (Workaround) Know your weakness but not motivated to fix it? Find a surrogate to use as a people workaround.** Similar to number 9, look at each critical weakness you identify and engage an internal or external person who is very good at that dimension to act in your behalf. Or delegate your weaknesses to your staff. Most of the time one or more on your staff will be better than you on several dimensions.

More Help?

In addition to the 10 tips listed for this dimension, there are some tips that may apply from *FYI For Your Improvement*™. We have coded each item to about 10 tips from the *FYI* book. To use this resource, the codes below refer to the chapter and then the tip number from the *FYI* book. For example, in item 17 below, 45-5 refers to Chapter 45 – Personal Learning, tip 5. If you don't have a copy of *FYI*, it is available through Lominger International at 952-345-3610 or www.lominger.com.

17. Seeks feedback.

45-5; 55-1,3,4,6; 104-1; 106-4; 108-1,2,7

44. Is insightful about personal mistakes and failures; learns from them and moves on.

44-7; 57-1,5,10; 104-1; 108-1,2,3,4,7

71. Have seen this person substantially change based upon critical feedback, making a mistake, or learning something new.

44-7; 45-5; 54-1,10; 104-1; 106-4; 108-1,2,3,7

Jobs That Would Add Skills in This Dimension

☐ Chair of Projects/Task Forces – requiring performing under tight deadlines and high visibility on an issue that matters to people higher up.

☐ Cross-Moves – requiring working with a new group of people from another function with a different background and viewpoint.

☐ Fix-Its/Turnarounds – requiring helping people rapidly change what they are doing and building their skills to be more successful.

☐ International Assignments – requiring conflicting cultures and a new and diverse population.

☐ Scope (complexity) Assignments – requiring communicating to a variety of people about a variety of topics.

Part-Time Assignments That Would Add Skills in This Dimension

☐ Make peace with an enemy or someone you've disappointed with a product or service or someone you've had some trouble with or don't get along with very well.

☐ Assemble a team of diverse people to accomplish a difficult task.

☐ Handle a tough negotiation with an internal or external client or customer.

☐ Take on a tough and previously undoable project where others have tried but failed to come up with the right answer.

☐ Help shut down a plant, office, product line, business, operation, etc.

☐ Attend a self-awareness workshop that has 360° and live feedback.

☐ Resolve a conflict between two people or two units.

☐ Integrate diverse systems, processes, or procedures across a decentralized or dispersed unit.

☐ Manage a dissatisfied internal or external customer; troubleshoot a performance or quality problem with a product or service.

☐ Lead a group through an unpopular change.

A man who has committed a mistake and doesn't correct it,
is committing another mistake.
Confucius (551 BCE - 479 BCE) – Chinese philosopher,
political figure, and educator

Suggested Readings

Brady, M. (2003). *Wisdom of listening*. Somerville, MA: Wisdom Publications.

Christian, K. (2004). *Your own worst enemy: Breaking the habit of adult underachievement*. New York, NY: Regan Books.

Folkman, J. R. (2006). *The power of feedback: 35 Principles for turning feedback from others into personal and professional change*. Hoboken, NJ: John Wiley & Sons.

Garber, P. R. (2004). *Giving and receiving performance feedback*. Amherst, MA: HRD Press.

Kirkland, K., & Manoojan, S. (2007). *Ongoing feedback: How to get it, how to use it*. Greensboro, NC: Center for Creative Leadership.

Lombardo, M. M., & Eichinger, R. W. (2009). *FYI for your improvement™: A guide for development and coaching – for learners, managers, mentors, and feedback givers* (5th ed.) Minneapolis, MN: Lominger International: A Korn/Ferry Company.

London, M. (2003). *Job feedback: Giving, seeking, and using feedback for performance improvement* (2nd ed.). Mahwah, NJ: Lawrence Erlbaum.

Pavlina, S. (2008). *Personal development for smart people: The conscious pursuit of personal growth*. Carlsbad, CA: Hay House.

Pedler, M., Burgoyne, J., & Boydell, T. (2007). *A manager's guide to self-development*. Berkshire, England: McGraw-Hill.

Thomas, R. J. (2008). *Crucibles of leadership: How to learn from experience to become a great leader*. Boston, MA: Harvard Business School Press.

Dimension 18
Role Flexibility

The wise adapt themselves to circumstances,
as water molds itself to the pitcher.
– Chinese proverb

Skilled

Behaves situationally; can move in many directions, play different roles, involve others or just act. Open to counter evidence.

Unskilled

May be seen as unbending; too much one-way—e.g., too participative or too directive.

Items

- [ ] 18. Is able to play different roles and act differently depending upon the demands of the situation; behaves situationally rather than how he/she feels or would like to act.
- [ ] 45. Has a good balance between following due processes (respecting the rights and needs of others) and just acting to get things done.
- [ ] 72. After stating a position and being presented with reasonable counter evidence, can change his/her mind.

Leadership Architect® Competencies Most Associated with This Dimension

Strong

- [ ] 2. *Dealing with* Ambiguity
- [ ] 12. Conflict Management
- [ ] 40. *Dealing with* Paradox
- [ ] 45. Personal Learning
- [ ] 46. Perspective

Moderate

- [ ] 31. Interpersonal Savvy
- [ ] 33. Listening
- [ ] 53. *Drive for* Results

Light

- ☐ 16. *Timely* Decision Making
- ☐ 39. Organizing
- ☐ 51. Problem Solving
- ☐ 56. Sizing Up People

Some Causes

- ☐ Always true to self
- ☐ Can't make smooth transitions
- ☐ Defensive
- ☐ Doesn't believe in playing multiple roles
- ☐ Doesn't read situations
- ☐ Doesn't shift roles easily or comfortably
- ☐ Not a good actor
- ☐ Not political
- ☐ One-trick pony
- ☐ Rigid and inflexible
- ☐ Single-tracked
- ☐ Stuck in the past

Developmental Difficulty

Moderate

The Map

Complex jobs in complex organizations demand that we play different roles. There is nothing chameleon-like or disingenuous about this. You need to lead and follow, be tough and be yielding. One way of acting isn't sufficient. The person who can honestly and credibly play the most roles generally gets more done and wins.

Some Remedies and Workarounds

- ☐ **1. Not shifting gears? Learn to transition comfortably between situations.** It's all in a day's work: going from a tense meeting to a celebration for a notable accomplishment. Think of your day as a series of transitions. For a week, monitor your gear-shifting behavior at work and at home. What transitions give you the most trouble? The least? Why? Practice gear-shifting transitions. On the way between activities, think about the transition you're making and the frame of mind required to make it.

- ☐ **2. Trouble finding balance? Work on acting in opposite ways.** Deliver a tough message but do it in a compassionate way. Dig into the details while trying to establish the conceptual drivers as well. Take a strong stand but listen and leave room for others to shine.

☐ 3. **Rely too much on favorite strengths? Pull back on overused skills.** Overdoing some of our strengths is typical. We push for results too hard; we analyze data too long; we try to be too nice. For our overdone behaviors, it's especially difficult to do the opposite. The key here is to balance what you do. If you're being too tough, stop and ask how the other person is doing. Ask yourself how you like to be treated. If you meddle, work on setting standards and outcomes. If you freeze under too much pressure, pause, take a drink of water, and ask yourself what is one productive thing you can do right now.

☐ 4. **Looking for a transition role model? Interview expert transitioners.** Talk with people who are good at making transitions, such as fix-it managers, shut-down managers, or excellent parents. Talk with an actor or actress; get to know people who have recently joined your organization from places quite different. Talk to a therapist who hears a different problem every hour.

☐ 5. **Easily readable? Recognize your triggers.** Initial anxious responses last 45 to 60 seconds. They are marked by your characteristic emotional response. Learn to recognize your triggers (raising your volume, drumming your fingers, shifting in your chair, etc.). Once you have figured out your triggers, ask why. Is it ego? Extra work? People you dislike or think are lazy? For each grouping, figure out what would be a more mature response. Learn to delay your response. Count to 10 or ask a clarifying question. Stall until the initial burst of glucose and adrenaline subsides.

☐ 6. **Used to being on the winning side of every argument? Start reducing conflict.** Trade with the other side, find points of agreement, make sure to understand their point of view, be problem oriented. Don't try to win every battle. Focus on common-ground issues, and treat each conflict as one that needs to be resolved with fairness for both sides.

☐ 7. **Not considering how your style affects others? Think more outside in.** What are the demands of this situation? Which of my approaches or styles will work best? Get out of your comfort zone of how you like to behave and consider the outside (customers, audience, person, group).

☐ 8. **(Workaround) Some style shifts out of reach? Use a surrogate.** Engage internal or external people who can play the roles you can't and delegate the tasks to them.

☐ 9. **(Workaround) Quantity of needed transitions overwhelming? Try to manage your schedule and time in single-role events.** One meeting, one agenda. One event, one role requirement. One group, one thing to do. Put a little time or break between different situations.

18

☐ 10. *(Workaround)* **Need to mentally rehearse style transitions? Think of yourself as an actor playing a number of roles.** An actor acts the role needed to make the play or movie work. Who they are is less important. Who they need to be is most important. Think about each key situation. How would Russell Crowe or Julia Roberts play the role? Body language? Voice? Pace? Process? Reactions? What are you trying to accomplish? What parts of you would work the best. See what works and what doesn't work. Maybe in time, you can actually become the parts you get good at.

More Help?

In addition to the 10 tips listed for this dimension, there are some tips that may apply from *FYI For Your Improvement*™. We have coded each item to about 10 tips from the *FYI* book. To use this resource, the codes below refer to the chapter and then the tip number from the *FYI* book. For example, in item 18 below, 40-1,2,3,5,6,7,9,10 refers to Chapter 40 – *Dealing with* Paradox, tips 1,2,3,5,6,7,9 and 10. If you don't have a copy of *FYI*, it is available through Lominger International at 952-345-3610 or www.lominger.com.

18. Is able to play different roles and act differently depending upon the demands of the situation; behaves situationally rather than how he/she feels or would like to act.

    40-1,2,3,5,6,7,9,10; 106-1,10

45. Has a good balance between following due processes (respecting the rights and needs of others) and just acting to get things done.

    1-2,3; 23-2; 33-6; 36-3; 40-2,3,10; 64-8; 104-4

72. After stating a position and being presented with reasonable counter evidence, can change his/her mind.

    12-1,5,7; 33-3; 37-1,2,4; 41-7; 104-4; 106-2

Jobs That Would Add Skills in This Dimension

☐ Chair of Projects/Task Forces – requiring performing under tight deadlines and high visibility on an issue that matters to people higher up.

☐ Cross-Moves – requiring working with a new group of people from another function with a different background and viewpoint.

☐ Fix-Its/Turnarounds – requiring helping people rapidly change what they are doing and building their skills to be more successful.

☐ International Assignments – requiring conflicting cultures and a new and diverse population.

☐ Scope (complexity) Assignments – requiring communicating to a variety of people about a variety of topics.

☐ Staff Leadership (influencing without authority) – working across organizational boundaries without the power to command attention where people and political skills are at a premium; conflict cannot be resolved with authority; influence is the main tool.

Part-Time Assignments That Would Add Skills in This Dimension

☐ Assemble a team of diverse people to accomplish a difficult task.

☐ Take on a tough and previously undoable project where others have tried but failed to come up with the right answer.

☐ Lead a group through an unpopular change.

☐ Form a multi-functional team to tackle a common issue.

☐ Manage the renovation of an office, floor, building, warehouse, etc.

☐ Help shut down a plant, office, product line, business, operation, etc.

☐ Make peace with an enemy or someone you've disappointed with a product or service or someone you've had some trouble with or don't get along with very well.

☐ Handle customer complaints and suggestions; troubleshoot a serious product or service breakdown.

☐ Represent to higher management the concerns of a group of non-exempt, clerical, administrative, or union employees to seek a resolution of a difficult issue.

☐ Take on a task or project you dislike or hate to do.

☐ Lobby for your organization on a contested issue in local, regional, state, federal, or an international government.

The art of life is a constant readjustment to our surroundings.
Okakura Kakuzo – Japanese scholar, author, and art critic

FACTOR II: PEOPLE AGILITY

18

Suggested Readings

Ashforth, B. (2000). *Role transitions in organizational life: An identity-based perspective*. Mahwah, NJ: Lawrence Erlbaum.

Bolton, R., & Bolton D. (2009). *People styles at work...And beyond: Making bad relationships good and good relationships better* (2nd ed.). New York, NY: AMACOM.

DiMitrius, J., & Mazzarella, W. (2008). *Reading people: How to understand people and predict their behavior—anytime, anyplace*. New York, NY: Random House.

Folkman, J. R. (2006). *The power of feedback: 35 Principles for turning feedback from others into personal and professional change*. Hoboken, NJ: John Wiley & Sons.

Gurvis, J., & Calarco, A. (2007). *Adaptability: Responding effectively to change*. Greensboro, NC: Center for Creative Leadership.

Levine, S. (2009). *Getting to resolution: Turning conflict into collaboration*. San Francisco, CA: Berrett-Koehler Publishers.

Nichols, M. (2009). *The lost art of listening: How learning to listen can improve relationships* (2nd ed.). New York, NY: Guilford Press.

Robinson, G., & Rose, M. (2004). *A leadership paradox: Influencing others by defining yourself*. Bloomington, IN: AuthorHouse.

Shea, G., & Gunther, R. E. (2008). *Your job survival guide: A manual for thriving in change*. Upper Saddle River, NJ: FT Press.

Vandergriff, D. (2006). *Raising the bar: Creating and nurturing adaptability to deal with the changing face of war*. Washington, DC: The Center for Defense Information.

Dimension 19
Self-Aware

The unexamined life is not worth living.
Socrates (469 BCE - 399 BCE) – Classical Greek philosopher

Skilled
Candid, knows what he/she is good and lousy at, not afraid to admit it and compensate; may be seen as humble and human, but might also be seen as too revealing by some.

Unskilled
Neither knows strengths and weaknesses nor discloses much; may be enigmatic, badly perceive his/her skill set, rush in where he/she should stay out.

Items
- ☐ 19. Understands his/her limits; compensates for what he/she isn't good at.
- ☐ 46. Candid to a fault about self, issues, and information (though not always with others who may be harmed).
- ☐ 73. Knows him/herself.

Leadership Architect® Competencies Most Associated with This Dimension

Strong
- ☐ 32. Learning on the Fly
- ☐ 44. Personal Disclosure
- ☐ 55. Self-Knowledge

Moderate
- ☐ 33. Listening
- ☐ 54. Self-Development
- ☐ 57. Standing Alone

Light
- ☐ 11. Composure
- ☐ 51. Problem Solving
- ☐ 56. Sizing Up People

113

Some Causes

☐ Blames others for own faults
☐ Defensive
☐ Doesn't ask for feedback
☐ Doesn't care what others think
☐ Doesn't listen
☐ Doesn't read people well
☐ Excessively high self-appraisal
☐ Fear of discovery of weaknesses
☐ Not ambitious
☐ Not curious

Developmental Difficulty

Moderate

The Map

People who don't know their strengths and weaknesses tend to overestimate themselves, a consistent finding in the research literature that has been related to both poor performance and being terminated. Knowing yourself helps you use your strengths better, compensate for what you're not good at, develop where you can, and avoid situations where you are unskilled. People who know themselves better do better.

Some Remedies and Workarounds

☐ 1. **Not used to personal reflection? Complete a self-inventory.** The goal of self-awareness is full knowledge. What are your clear strengths and how can you use them better? What do you overdo? What are strengths you have been previously unaware of? What are known weaknesses? What are untested areas? And most important, what are your blind spots, those areas in which you see yourself as much more skilled than others see you. It is blind spots above all else that stall careers.

☐ 2. **Unclear how others see you? Get more feedback.** 360° feedback—where you compare your responses on a set of competencies to those of boss, peers, direct reports (if any), and sometimes customers—is the preferred approach. Many other avenues are open to you as well—boss, confidantes, or a development partner if you're lucky enough to have one.

☐ 3. **Not sure which strengths and weaknesses to focus on? Focus on the highest and lowest ratings from each group.** Don't spend time worrying about whether your scores are high or low in an absolute sense. 360° instruments aren't designed as performance assessments ordinarily.

For development, you should worry about you relative to you. What are your highest and lowest ratings?

☐ **4. Looking for root causes? Ask why.** Why am I seen this way? How did my strengths get to be so? Are my weaknesses things I avoid, things I'm simply not skilled at, things I dislike or things I've never done? What experiences shaped my pattern? Do I have strengths that are related to my weaknesses, such as the smart person who makes others feel less so? Use this analysis to determine what is relatively easier and tougher for you to do.

☐ **5. Some behaviors more troubling to you than others? Solicit written feedback.** Prepare specific areas you are concerned about and ask people to respond in writing. Ask them what they would like to see you keep doing, start doing, stop doing, or do differently. If you know the people well, you can try face-to-face feedback, although you should know that this is usually blander and more positive than written feedback. If you do this, select specific areas and state what you think the issue or need for improvement is. Don't ask general questions. Get them to respond to your statements.

☐ **6. Seen as arrogant and/or defensive? Be open to all feedback.** Many people with a need in this area are seen as self-sufficient and disinterested in feedback and change. If this is the case, you may have to ask repeatedly. And regardless of the feedback, accept it. Don't say it's inaccurate or a one-time failing; don't argue or qualify. Just take it in. Use mental rehearsal to get ready for what may happen. If you comment at all, give examples of the behavior being described to validate what they are saying. Chances are good they are right. Defensive and arrogant people typically have major blind spots.

☐ **7. Has perception become reality? Show your true intent through action.** Even if the feedback is not true, you need to deal with it. If people, especially those above you, believe these things, your career will be damaged. You need to construct a plan to convince people of the untruth(s) by deeds, not words. Plan how you will act in critical situations and expect it to take quite a while for people to see you differently. It may take 10 times before people reconsider their view of you.

☐ **8. Afraid to admit shortcomings? Disclose more.** If you deny, minimize, or excuse away mistakes and shortcomings, take a chance and admit that you're imperfect like everyone else. Let your inside thoughts out in the open more often. Sprinkle normal work conversation with doubts, what you're thinking about, and what's getting in the way. Since you probably don't know how to do this, select three people who are good at admitting mistakes and shortcomings and observe how they do it.

19

☐ 9. **Are some of your weaknesses chronic? Seek to neutralize the negatives.** You can compensate for your flat spots and downsides. All of us are poor at some things and beating on them is counterproductive. If you've failed or been lackluster in an area repeatedly, you can change jobs, restructure your job, or simply work to neutralize the downside.

☐ 10. *(Workaround)* **Need to start small? Make it a goal to know yourself completely without worrying about doing anything about your weaknesses.** Ask everyone you respect. Do a 360° feedback assessment. Research has shown that just knowing about all of your weaknesses can actually lead to some improvement without actually working on them. Look at each critical weakness you identify and engage an internal or external person who is very good at that competency to act in your behalf. Or delegate your weaknesses to your staff. Most of the time one or more on your staff will be better than you on several competencies.

More Help?

In addition to the 10 tips listed for this dimension, there are some tips that may apply from *FYI For Your Improvement*™. We have coded each item to about 10 tips from the *FYI* book. To use this resource, the codes below refer to the chapter and then the tip number from the *FYI* book. For example, in item 19 below, 44-6,7 refers to Chapter 44 – Personal Disclosure, tips 6 and 7. If you don't have a copy of *FYI*, it is available through Lominger International at 952-345-3610 or www.lominger.com.

19. Understands his/her limits; compensates for what he/she isn't good at.

   44-6,7; 54-7; 55-1,3; 104-1,2; 108-1,4,7

46. Candid to a fault about self, issues, and information (though not always with others who may be harmed).

   44-1,2,3,4,5,6,7,8,9,10

73. Knows him/herself.

   55-1,2,3,4,5,6,7,8,9,10

Jobs That Would Add Skills in This Dimension

☐ Chair of Projects/Task Forces – requiring performing under tight deadlines and high visibility on an issue that matters to people higher up.

☐ Cross-Moves – requiring working with a new group of people from another function with a different background and viewpoint.

☐ International Assignments – requiring conflicting cultures and a new and diverse population.

☐ Scope (complexity) Assignments – requiring communicating to a variety of new people about a variety of topics.

☐ Staff Leadership (influencing without authority) – working across organizational boundaries without the power to command attention where people and political skills are at a premium; conflict cannot be resolved with authority; influence is the main tool.

☐ Start-Ups – requiring forging a new team and building new skills as you go.

Part-Time Assignments That Would Add Skills in This Dimension

☐ Make peace with an enemy or someone you've disappointed with a product or service or someone you've had some trouble with or don't get along with very well.

☐ Attend a self-awareness workshop that has 360° and live feedback.

☐ Take on a tough and previously undoable project where others have tried but failed to come up with the right answer.

☐ Assemble a team of diverse people to accomplish a difficult task.

☐ Handle customer complaints and suggestions.

☐ Help shut down a plant, office, product line, business, operation, etc.

☐ Try to learn something new, fun, or frivolous to see how good you can get (e.g., juggling, square dancing, magic).

☐ Work with a mentor and review all past assessments you have had and can remember, and summarize who you are and what that means for the rest of your career.

☐ Attend a course or an event which will push you beyond your usual limits and is outside your comfort zone (e.g., Outward Bound, language immersion training, sensitivity group, Toastmasters, clown school).

☐ Join a self-help or support group.

19

A man who knows he is a fool is not a great fool.
Chuang-tzu (370 BCE - 301 BCE) – Chinese philosopher

Suggested Readings

Allen, R. (2003). *The playful way to knowing yourself: A creative workbook to inspire self-discovery.* New York, NY: Houghton Mifflin Company.

Cashman, K. (2008). *Leadership from the inside out: Becoming a leader for life* (2nd ed.). San Francisco, CA: Berrett-Koehler Publishers.

Folkman, J. R. (2006). *The power of feedback: 35 Principles for turning feedback from others into personal and professional change.* Hoboken, NJ: John Wiley & Sons.

George, B. (with Sims, P.). (2007). *True north: Discover your authentic leadership.* San Francisco, CA: Jossey-Bass.

Goldsmith, M., & Reiter, M. (2007). *What got you here won't get you there: How successful people become even more successful.* New York, NY: Hyperion.

Jerred, F. (2006). *Understand the true self: The treasure within.* Victoria, Canada: Trafford Publishing.

Leider, R. J., & Shapiro, D. A. (2001). *Whistle while you work: Heeding your life's calling.* San Francisco, CA: Berrett-Koehler Publishers.

Lombardo, M. M., & Eichinger, R. W. (2004). *The leadership machine.* Minneapolis, MN: Lominger International: A Korn/Ferry Company.

McLeod, A. (2007). *Self-coaching leadership: Simple steps from managers to leader.* Chichester, England: John Wiley & Sons.

Pavlina, S. (2008). *Personal development for smart people: The conscious pursuit of personal growth.* Carlsbad, CA: Hay House.

Pearman, R. R., Lombardo, M. M., & Eichinger, R. W. (2005). *You: Being more effective in your MBTI® type.* Minneapolis, MN: Lominger International: A Korn/Ferry Company.

Pedler, M., Burgoyne, J., & Boydell, T. (2007). *A manager's guide to self-development.* Berkshire, England: McGraw-Hill.

Factor III
Change Agility

High
People high on this Factor like to tinker with ideas and put them into practice. They are likely to be highly interested in continuous improvements. They are cool under pressure and can handle the heat and consequences of being in the vanguard of change efforts.

Low
People low on this Factor may like things ordered and as usual. They may be uncomfortable with experimentation. Liking sameness, they may appear resistant or disinterested in innovation or the tinkering and conflict management required to make it work. At the extreme, they might be seen as perfectionists who try to get everything just so, thereby insulating themselves from criticism.

Some Causes
- ☐ Avoids conflict
- ☐ Dislikes the noise of change
- ☐ Doesn't want to lead
- ☐ Fear of criticism
- ☐ Fear of failing in the new
- ☐ Fear of uncertainty
- ☐ Gets easily stressed and anxious
- ☐ Not curious
- ☐ Not experimental
- ☐ Perfectionist
- ☐ Prefers predictability
- ☐ Quiet, unchanging past
- ☐ Too comfortable
- ☐ Wed to the past

119

III

Dimension 20
Experimenter

I haven't failed, I've found 10,000 ways that don't work.
Thomas Edison – U. S. scientist and inventor

Skilled
Likes test cases—ideas, products, services; fiddles with things to improve something or to come up with a creative solution; comfortable trying several times before finding the right solution.

Unskilled
Likes to have everything just so; may resist the new, criticizing its inevitable imperfections; may call experimentation sloppiness, and hold changes up to impossibly mature standards.

Items
- ☐ 20. Is an inveterate tinkerer; can't leave things alone for long without seeking a new way.
- ☐ 47. Is creative and innovative.
- ☐ 74. Floats trial balloons, tries products and services not quite ready, serves up preliminary thinking, all in the service of a better final product.

Leadership Architect® Competencies Most Associated with This Dimension

Strong
- ☐ 2. *Dealing with* Ambiguity
- ☐ 14. Creativity
- ☐ 28. Innovation Management
- ☐ 32. Learning on the Fly
- ☐ 51. Problem Solving

Moderate
- ☐ 46. Perspective
- ☐ 61. Technical Learning

20

Light

☐ 1. Action Oriented
☐ 16. *Timely* Decision Making
☐ 40. *Dealing with* Paradox

Some Causes

☐ Avoids conflict
☐ Can't think of anything new or different
☐ Comfortable with what is
☐ Defensive
☐ Doesn't like taking risks
☐ Doesn't like to be out front in the lead
☐ Fear of failure and making mistakes
☐ Impatient
☐ Not curious
☐ Perfectionist
☐ Slow
☐ Withdrawn and quiet

Developmental Difficulty

Easier

The Map

The more experiments, the more chances to learn to do something better. Too often we do things the same old way, yet expect a different outcome. Trial and error eventually leads to improvement. Most of the things we use today in life were not created instantly. Instead, they came along as the very last car in a long experimenting train.

Some Remedies and Workarounds

☐ **1. Perfectionist? Trust your intuition.** Learn to recognize it for what it is—collecting all the information to improve confidence and avoid criticism. Anyone with a brain and 100% of the information will make good decisions, but others are doing it with far less. When in the process of trying to solve something, try writing down what you would do at various points along the way. Then revisit it each time you gain more information. At what point would you have made the same decision as you did with all or more of the information? Most of the time, you could have settled upon a solution long before you actually did. Many of us wait an extra week or two, but our decision doesn't change.

☐ **2. Afraid? Treat failures and mistakes as chances to learn.** Successful executives report more failures and mistakes than do the less successful. You can't learn from things you're not doing. The key is to make small decisions, get instant feedback, correct, and get better. Getting it right the first time is not likely. Be an incrementalist. Triple your learning opportunities by trying three small experiments.

☐ **3. Comfortable? Get away from your favorite solutions.** They interfere with growth and change. Decide what you would most likely do, then don't do it. Carve out some time—talk with others, look for parallels in other organizations, talk to an expert in an unrelated field, pick some unusual or odd facts about the problem you're facing and see what they signal, brainstorm with a one-time problem-solving group. Don't restrict your solution space.

☐ **4. Frustrated? Accept that most innovations fail.** The most successful innovators do it by sheer quantity and learning from failure. Edison took 3,000 shots at the lightbulb. Try lots of quick, low-impact experiments to increase the chances of success. For example, try five ways to test a product rather than one big carefully planned one. Look for something common in the failure that is never present when there is a success. Let the plan evolve from the tests.

☐ **5. Adhering to norms? Challenge the status quo.** Creativity requires combining two things previously unconnected or changing how we look at them. It also requires generating ideas without judging them initially. People who do this well are atypical as well—they may be playful, contrary, and averse to many rules. You may have to buffer them somewhat and give them some room. You won't get anything new by following the normal set-a-goal-and-time-schedule approach.

☐ **6. Risk averse? Up your risk comfort by letting others experiment.** Delegate more; pick some small things you do right. Pick an easy piece of a larger project, then pick a couple of tougher pieces. Review each one to see what went well and not well.

☐ **7. Lacking boldness? Tap into your passion.** If you're tired of what you're doing, find something for which you have enthusiasm. Appoint yourself as champion. Throw out trial balloons to see if your notion spurs some interest. Find an experimenter to go in with you. Bring in a heavy expert. Plant seeds at every opportunity.

☐ **8. *(Workaround)* Not motivated to experiment? Leverage others' skills.** While not interested or willing to be creative and innovative yourself, give others around you the freedom to run. Delegate experimentation. Don't resist. Don't be a critic. Don't get in the way.

20

☐ 9. *(Workaround)* **Not enough time? Use your network.** Engage internal and external resources who are creative, innovative, and who like to experiment. Let them identify the most likely areas for the new and different.

☐ 10. *(Workaround)* **Lacking critical skills? Get reinforcement.** Get help if you are not a change manager. Use an internal or external consultant who specializes in planning for and managing change. Or delegate it to your staff. Let them plan for and manage the change.

More Help?

In addition to the 10 tips listed for this dimension, there are some tips that may apply from *FYI For Your Improvement*™. We have coded each item to about 10 tips from the *FYI* book. To use this resource, the codes below refer to the chapter and then the tip number from the *FYI* book. For example, in item 20 below, 1-3,5 refers to Chapter 1 – Action Oriented, tips 3 and 5. If you don't have a copy of *FYI*, it is available through Lominger International at 952-345-3610 or www.lominger.com.

20. Is an inveterate tinkerer; can't leave things alone for long without seeking a new way.

1-3,5; 2-1,3,6; 14-1,4; 32-4,9; 51-2

47. Is creative and innovative.

14-1,2,3,4,5,9,10; 28-2,3,4

74. Floats trial balloons, tries products and services not quite ready, serves up preliminary thinking, all in the service of a better final product.

1-3; 2-1,2,7; 16-7; 32-3,4,9; 57-1,9

Jobs That Would Add Skills in This Dimension

☐ Crisis Manager or Change Manager – requiring resourceful decisions under tight time pressure with a low level of consultation.

☐ Fix-Its/Turnarounds – requiring making tough decisions impacting a variety of people and constituencies and trying a lot of new things.

☐ International Assignments – requiring communicating to a new and diverse population and taking first-time actions in a new environment.

☐ Scope (complexity) Assignments – requiring a variety of initiatives about a variety of topics in areas new to the person.

☐ Start-Ups – requiring forging a new team and trying a variety of new and first-time initiatives on a tight timetable.

20

Part-Time Assignments That Would Add Skills in This Dimension

☐ Relaunch an existing product or service that's not doing well by trying things not tried before.

☐ Assemble a team of diverse people to accomplish a difficult task.

☐ Manage a group of people working on a fix-it or turnaround situation or project.

☐ Take on a tough and undoable project, one where others who have tried it have failed.

☐ Launch a new product, service, or process.

☐ Build a multi-functional project team to tackle a common business issue or problem.

☐ Plan a new site for a building (plant, field office, headquarters, etc.).

☐ Handle a tough negotiation with an internal or external client or customer.

☐ Take on a task you dislike or hate to do.

☐ Work on a team that has to integrate diverse systems (move from using five computer platforms into one), processes (integrating a distinct, stand-alone, quality-assurance process into a product development process), or procedures (five competency models into one) across decentralized and/or dispersed units where you have to find the most common solution.

A life spent making mistakes is not only more honorable, but more useful than a life spent doing nothing.
George Bernard Shaw – Irish playwright, literary critic, and Nobel Prize and Oscar winner

20

Suggested Readings

Anthony, S. D., Johnson, M. W., Sinfield, J. V., & Altman, E. J. (2008). *Innovator's guide to growth: Putting disruptive innovation to work*. Boston, MA: Harvard Business School Press.

Antony, M. M., & Swinson, R. P. (2009). *When perfect isn't good enough: Strategies for coping with perfectionism* (2nd ed.). Oakland, CA: New Harbinger Publications, Inc.

Axelrod, A. (2008). *Edison on innovation: 102 Lessons in creativity for business and beyond*. San Francisco, CA: Jossey-Bass.

FACTOR III: CHANGE AGILITY

Davila, T., Epstein, M. J., & Shelton, R. (2005). *Making innovation work: How to manage it, measure it, and profit from it.* Philadelphia: Wharton School Publishing.

De Bono, E. (1993). *Serious creativity: Using the power of lateral thinking to create new ideas.* New York, NY: HarperBusiness.

Drucker, P. F. (2006). *Innovation and entrepreneurship.* New York, NY: HarperCollins.

Futurist Magazine. http://www.wfs.org.

Gelb, M., & Caldicott, S. M. (2007). *Innovate like Edison: The success system of America's greatest inventor.* New York, NY: Dutton.

Hamel, G. (with Breen, B.). (2007). *The future of management.* Boston, MA: Harvard Business School Press.

Hamel, G., & Prahalad, C. K. (1996). *Competing for the future.* Boston, MA: Harvard Business School Press.

Kanter, R. M., Kao, J., & Wiersema, F. (Eds.). (1997). *Innovation: Breakthrough thinking at 3M, DuPont, GE, Pfizer and Rubbermaid.* New York, NY: HarperCollins Publishers.

Kidder, T. (1981). *The soul of a new machine.* Boston, MA: Little, Brown and Co.

Kotter, J. P. (1996). *Leading change.* Boston, MA: Harvard Business School Press.

Kotter, J. P. (2008). *A sense of urgency.* Boston, MA: Harvard Business Press.

Kotter, J. P., & Cohen, D. S. (2002). *The heart of change: Real-life stories of how people change their organizations.* Boston, MA: Harvard Business School Press.

Kotter, J. P., & Rathgeber, H. (2006). *Our iceberg is melting: Changing and succeeding under any conditions.* New York, NY: St. Martin's Press.

O'Sullivan, D., & Dooley, L. (2008). *Applying innovation.* Thousand Oaks, CA: Sage Publications.

Thomas, R. J. (2008). *Crucibles of leadership: How to learn from experience to become a great leader.* Boston, MA: Harvard Business School Press.

Torbert, W. R. (2004). *Action inquiry: The secret of timely and transforming leadership.* San Francisco, CA: Berrett-Koehler Publishers.

20

Dimension 21
Innovation Manager

Innovation distinguishes between a leader and a follower.
Steve Jobs – U.S. entrepreneur and co-founder of Apple and Pixar

Skilled
Can manage ideas so they become practice; can move ideas to market; is both team and organizationally savvy.

Unskilled
Has problems with implementing ideas; may have trouble with the process of innovation, getting ideas to fruition in a team, or getting things done in an organizational setting.

Items
- ☐ 21. Can manage a team from idea to implementation.
- ☐ 48. Can personally take an innovative idea and move it all the way to practice.
- ☐ 75. Knows how to get things done outside of formal channels as well as within them; is savvy about whom to go to, and when.

Leadership Architect® Competencies Most Associated with This Dimension

Strong
- ☐ 28. Innovation Management
- ☐ 38. Organizational Agility
- ☐ 39. Organizing
- ☐ 52. Process Management

Moderate
- ☐ 36. Motivating Others
- ☐ 37. Negotiating

21

Light

- ☐ 2. *Dealing with* Ambiguity
- ☐ 12. Conflict Management
- ☐ 20. Directing Others
- ☐ 47. Planning
- ☐ 51. Problem Solving

Some Causes

- ☐ A loner
- ☐ Avoids conflict
- ☐ Dislikes risk
- ☐ Doesn't like to be out front leading
- ☐ Impatient
- ☐ Likes to be right
- ☐ Not creative
- ☐ Not inspiring
- ☐ Not politically savvy
- ☐ Not resourceful
- ☐ Not well networked
- ☐ Not well organized
- ☐ Shy and withdrawn
- ☐ Too comfortable with what is

Developmental Difficulty

Moderate

21

The Map

Thinking through and managing innovation is different from ordinary planning and execution. It requires understanding the creative process and the high failure rates associated with innovation. Growth and progress ride on the back of innovation. Being able to find and then implement the new, different, and the unique drives progress.

Some Remedies

- ☐ **1. Not connecting with your customer base? Understand your markets.** What have your customers done in the past? What have your competitors done successfully? Which new products or services failed and which succeeded? Why? Talk to the strategic planners in your organization. Access experts. Talk to key customers. Consult your team.

☐ **2. Frustrated? Accept that most innovations fail.** The most successful innovators do it by sheer quantity and learning from failure. Edison took 3,000 shots at the lightbulb. Try lots of quick, inexpensive experiments to increase the chances of success. For example, try five ways to test a product rather than one big carefully planned one. Look for something common in the failure that is never present when there is a success. Let the plan evolve from the tests.

☐ **3. Afraid? Treat failures and mistakes as chances to learn.** Successful executives report more failures and mistakes than do the less successful. You can't learn from things you're not doing. The key is to make small decisions, get instant feedback, correct, and get better. Getting it right the first time is not likely. Be an incrementalist. Triple your learning opportunities by trying three small experiments.

☐ **4. Adhering to norms? Challenge the status quo.** Creativity requires combining two things previously unconnected or changing how we look at them. It also requires generating ideas without judging them initially. People who do this well are atypical as well—they may be playful, contrary, and averse to many rules. You may have to buffer them somewhat and give them some room. You won't get anything new by following the normal set-a-goal-and-time-schedule approach.

☐ **5. No breakthrough ideas? Ask more questions.** Solutions typically outweigh questions eight to one in problem-solving meetings. Have the group ask more questions and spend half its time really looking at a problem statement. Have the group take a product/service you are dissatisfied with and represent it visually—flowchart it or use a series of pictures. Cut it up into its component pieces and reorder them. Ask how you could combine three pieces into one. Look for patterns. Pull in fresh thinking into the group (use customers, people who know nothing about the area). Many studies have shown that the more diverse the group, the fresher the thinking. Creativity starts with lots of ideas and thorough examination of the problem.

☐ **6. Lacking support? Make a compelling case.** Innovation is often like an orphan in an organization. Early in the process, resources will probably be tight. You will have to deal with other units and detractors. Be prepared to state the value again and again. What problem will it solve? How can it help the organization or other units? Think carefully about whom to go to and how to gain support. Appeal to the common good, trade something, and work to minimize negative effects on others. Work from the outside in. Determine the demands and interests of groups and individuals and appeal to those.

21

☐ **7. Giving up too soon on an idea? Try a different approach.** If you have trouble going back the second or third time, then switch approaches. For example, you could meet with all stakeholders, a single key stakeholder, present the idea to a group, call in an expert to buttress your innovation, or project various scenarios showing the value of the idea.

☐ **8. Losing support? Inspire your team.** Innovation is tougher than work-as-usual. Celebrate wins, measure progress in small steps, have members of the group present promising results, establish common cause, reinforce often why this is important, set small checkpoints and little goals, and treat failures as exciting chances to learn how to do it better.

☐ **9. *(Workaround)* Lacking critical skills? Get reinforcement.** Acknowledge your weaknesses and delegate them to your staff to plan and do. Give them room to run. Be sure to look for innovators when adding people to your team.

☐ **10. *(Workaround)* Not enough time? Use your network.** Engage internal or external experts in managing innovation. Let them plan and help you execute.

More Help?

In addition to the 10 tips listed for this dimension, there are some tips that may apply from *FYI For Your Improvement*™. We have coded each item to about 10 tips from the *FYI* book. To use this resource, the codes below refer to the chapter and then the tip number from the *FYI* book. For example, in item 21 below, 28-1,2,3,4,6,7,8,9,10 refers to Chapter 28 – Innovation Management, tips 1,2,3,4,6,7,8,9 and 10. If you don't have a copy of *FYI*, it is available through Lominger International at 952-345-3610 or www.lominger.com.

21. Can manage a team from idea to implementation.

    28-1,2,3,4,6,7,8,9,10; 60-1

48. Can personally take an innovative idea and move it all the way to practice.

    28-1,7,8,9,10; 43-1; 57-1,3,7,9

75. Knows how to get things done outside of formal channels as well as within them; is savvy about whom to go to, and when.

    38-4,8,9,10; 42-1,5; 48-2,3,9; 64-8

21

Jobs That Would Add Skills in This Dimension

☐ Chair of Projects/Task Forces – requiring finding new and effective solutions under tight deadlines and high visibility on an issue that matters to people higher up.

☐ Fix-Its/Turnarounds – requiring trying new things to change the situation around where others have failed.

☐ Line to Staff Switches – requiring addressing a new group of people with different functional homes and a different viewpoint on the world with new and different solutions.

☐ Scope (complexity) Assignments – requiring working on a variety of initiatives across diverse areas.

☐ Start-Ups – requiring forging a new team and trying things for the first time on a tight timetable.

Part-Time Assignments That Would Add Skills in This Dimension

☐ Relaunch an existing product or service that's not doing well.

☐ Manage a group of people involved in tackling a fix-it or turnaround project.

☐ Integrate diverse systems, processes, or procedures across decentralized and/or dispersed units.

☐ Build a multi-functional project team to tackle a common business issue or problem.

☐ Launch a new product, service, or process.

☐ Manage a group of people in a rapidly expanding operation.

☐ Take on a tough and undoable project, one where others who have tried it have failed.

☐ Manage a group through a significant business crisis.

☐ Plan for and start up something small (secretarial pool, athletic program, suggestion system, program, etc.).

☐ Plan an off-site meeting, conference, convention, trade show event, etc.

Mindless habitual behavior is the enemy of innovation.
Rosabeth Moss Kanter – U. S. management scholar

21

FACTOR III: CHANGE AGILITY

21

Suggested Readings

Adair, J. (2009). *Leadership for innovation: How to organize team creativity and harvest ideas*. Philadelphia: Kogan Page.

Anthony, S. D., Johnson, M. W., Sinfield, J. V., & Altman, E. J. (2008). *Innovator's guide to growth: Putting disruptive innovation to work*. Boston, MA: Harvard Business School Press.

Bossidy, L., & Charan, R. (with Burck, C.). (2002). *Execution: The discipline of getting things done*. New York, NY: Crown Business.

Chesbrough, H. (2006). *Open business models: How to thrive in the new innovation landscape*. Boston, MA: Harvard Business School Press.

Davila, T., Epstein, M. J., & Shelton, R. (2005). *Making innovation work: How to manage it, measure it, and profit from it*. Philadelphia: Wharton School Publishing.

Deschamp, J. P. (2008). *Innovation leaders: How senior executives stimulate, steer and sustain innovation*. West Sussex, England: John Wiley & Sons, Ltd.

Drucker, P. F. (2006). *Innovation and entrepreneurship*. New York, NY: HarperCollins.

Futurist Magazine. http://www.wfs.org.

Hamel, G. (with Breen, B.). (2007). *The future of management*. Boston, MA: Harvard Business School Press.

Hamel, G., & Prahalad, C. K. (1996). *Competing for the future*. Boston, MA: Harvard Business School Press.

Hansen, M. T., & Birkinshaw, J. (2008). The innovation chain. *Harvard Business Review, 85*, 121-130.

Heath, C., & Heath, D. (2007). *Made to stick: Why some ideas survive and others die*. New York, NY: Random House.

Horibe, F. (2008). *Creating the innovation culture: Leveraging visionaries, dissenters and other useful troublemakers*. Etobicoke, ON: John Wiley & Sons Canada Ltd.

Jamrog, J., Vickers, M., & Bear, D. (2006). Building and sustaining a culture that supports innovation. *Human Resource Planning, 29*(3), 9-19.

Kanter, R. M., Kao, J., & Wiersema, F. (Eds.). (1997). *Innovation: Breakthrough thinking at 3M, DuPont, GE, Pfizer and Rubbermaid*. New York, NY: HarperCollins Publishers.

Kidder, T. (1981). *The soul of a new machine*. Boston, MA: Little, Brown and Co.

Koch, R. (1998). *The 80/20 principle: The secret of achieving more with less.* New York, NY: Doubleday.

Kotter, J. P. (1996). *Leading change.* Boston, MA: Harvard Business School Press.

Kotter, J. P., & Cohen, D. S. (2002). *The heart of change: Real-life stories of how people change their organizations.* Boston, MA: Harvard Business School Press.

Lafley, A.G., & Charan, R. (2008). *The game-changer: How you can drive revenue and profit growth with innovation.* New York, NY: Crown Business.

O'Sullivan, D., & Dooley, L. (2008). *Applying innovation.* Thousand Oaks, CA: Sage Publications.

Phillips, J. (2008). *Make us more innovative: Critical factors for innovation success.* Lincoln, NE: iUniverse.

Sawyer, K. (2008). *Group genius: The creative power of collaboration.* New York, NY: Basic Books.

Sloane, P. (2007). *The innovative leader: How to inspire your team and drive creativity.* Philadelphia: Kogan Page.

The Systems Thinker®. http://www.thesystemsthinker.com.

21

21

Dimension 22
Taking the Heat

Courage is resistance to fear, mastery of fear, not absence of fear.
Mark Twain – American humorist, satirist, lecturer, and writer

Skilled
Philosophical about personal attacks; knows that people will be upset by change, negative consequences are possible; goes ahead with change.

Unskilled
May fold up under pressure or in the face of being in trouble with people; may try too hard to please everyone; may simply avoid such situations.

Items
- ☐ 22. Knows that change is unsettling; can take a lot of heat, even when it gets personal.
- ☐ 49. Doesn't let others' reactions to his/her mistakes and failures be a deterrent to going ahead if he/she thinks something will eventually work.
- ☐ 76. Lives with negative consequences of being ahead of others on change.

Leadership Architect® Competencies Most Associated with This Dimension

Strong
- ☐ 2. *Dealing with* Ambiguity
- ☐ 11. Composure
- ☐ 12. Conflict Management
- ☐ 57. Standing Alone

Moderate
- ☐ 9. Command Skills
- ☐ 41. Patience
- ☐ 43. Perseverance
- ☐ 65. *Managing* Vision and Purpose

22

Light

- ☐ 26. Humor
- ☐ 33. Listening
- ☐ 34. Managerial Courage
- ☐ 37. Negotiating
- ☐ 40. *Dealing with* Paradox

Some Causes

- ☐ Avoids conflict
- ☐ Avoids criticism
- ☐ Cares a lot about what people think
- ☐ Comfortable with the way things are
- ☐ Defensive
- ☐ Doesn't like to be first
- ☐ Doesn't listen
- ☐ Gets easily upset
- ☐ Impatient with others not up-to-speed
- ☐ Not well networked
- ☐ Perfectionist
- ☐ Prefers to share responsibility
- ☐ Stops if there is resistance
- ☐ Takes criticism personally

Developmental Difficulty

Moderate

22

The Map

To be a change champion, you have to be ready to pull some arrows from various places, including your back. Change is scary, frustrating, and anxiety-producing for many. One reaction is to attack the change agent directly or, more likely, indirectly. Sabotage is common. All of this is natural. We are comfort-zone, nest-building organisms. We like things to stay the same. Those who try to mess with our comfort zone will feel our wrath. Successful change agents know this and absorb and chill unproductive noise by continuing to move forward.

Some Remedies and Workarounds

- ☐ 1. **Wary of criticism? Prepare in advance.** Leading is risky. You have to defend what you're doing, so convince yourself first that you are on the right track. Be prepared to explain again and again, to attract lightning bolts from detractors, from those unsettled by change and from those who will always say it could have been done differently, better, and cheaper. To prepare for this, think about the 10 objections that will come up and mentally rehearse how you will reply. Listen patiently to people's concerns, acknowledge them, then explain why you think the change will be beneficial. Attack positions, but not people.

☐ **2. Losing your composure? Recognize your triggers.** Initial anxious responses last 45 to 60 seconds. They are marked by your characteristic emotional response. Learn to recognize your triggers (raising your volume, drumming your fingers, shifting in your chair, etc.). Once you have figured out your triggers, ask why. Is it ego? Extra work? People you dislike or think are lazy? For each grouping, figure out what would be a more mature response. Learn to delay your response. Count to 10 or ask a clarifying question. Stall until the initial burst of glucose and adrenaline subsides.

☐ **3. Afraid? Embrace mistakes.** Expect trouble and admit that 20% to 50% of the time will be spent debugging, fixing mistakes, and figuring out what went wrong. Treat each one as a chance to learn. It's a work in progress.

☐ **4. Controlling? Give others choices.** How changes should be made should be as open as possible. Your job is the what and the why. Studies show that people work harder when they have a sense of choice over how they accomplish the new and different.

☐ **5. Always battling with others? Keep conflicts small.** Find out what the points of agreement are rather than focusing on the disagreements only. Don't resort to general statements such as "We have trust problems with your unit." Keep the concern specific—stick to whats and whens.

☐ **6. What if you're attacked? Stay calm.** Let the other side vent, but don't react directly or instantly. Pause. Listen. Nod. Ask clarifying questions. Ask open-ended questions like "What could I do to help?" Restate their position so they know you've heard them. You don't have to do anything to appease; just listen and accept that they are irritated. Your goal is to calm the situation so you can get back to more reasonable discussion.

☐ **7. Lacking boldness? Tap into your passion.** If you're tired of what you're doing, find something for which you have enthusiasm. Appoint yourself as the change champion. Throw out trial balloons to see if your notion spurs some interest. Find an experimenter to go in with you. Bring in a heavy expert. Plant seeds at every opportunity.

22

☐ **8. Give up too soon on an idea? Try different approaches.** If you have trouble going back the second or third time, then switch approaches. For example, you could meet with all stakeholders, a single key stakeholder, present the idea to a group, call in an expert to buttress your innovation, or project various scenarios showing the value of the idea.

☐ **9. Dealing with persistent naysayers? Deliver an ultimatum.** At the end game, sometimes, try as you might, nothing works. The detractors are recalcitrant. Then, rarely, you may have to pull someone aside and say, "I've heard all your worries and have tried to respond to them. Now I'm moving on. Are you on or off the train?"

☐ **10. *(Workaround)* Low threshold for criticism? Share the heat.** If it's just not in your nature to take the heat of leading change, use a participative strategy. Spread it so if there is heat, everyone gets just a bit warm. Get the affected people together to scope out the need, plan for and execute the change. You will give up some control and things may not be done exactly as you would like.

More Help?

In addition to the 10 tips listed for this dimension, there are some tips that may apply from *FYI For Your Improvement*™. We have coded each item to about 10 tips from the *FYI* book. To use this resource, the codes below refer to the chapter and then the tip number from the *FYI* book. For example, in item 22 below, 2-1 refers to Chapter 2 – *Dealing with* Ambiguity, tip 1. If you don't have a copy of *FYI*, it is available through Lominger International at 952-345-3610 or www.lominger.com.

22. Knows that change is unsettling; can take a lot of heat, even when it gets personal.
    2-1; 12-3,4; 57-1,2,4,6,7; 65-3,7

49. Doesn't let others' reactions to his/her mistakes and failures be a deterrent to going ahead if he/she thinks something will eventually work.
    12-3,4; 57-1,2,3,5,6,7,8,9

76. Lives with negative consequences of being ahead of others on change.
    2-1; 12-3,4; 57-1,4,5,6,7; 65-3,7

Jobs That Would Add Skills in This Dimension

☐ Crisis Manager or Change Manager – requiring tough-minded decisions under tight time pressure with a low level of consultation and high visibility.

☐ Fix-Its/Turnarounds – requiring making tough decisions impacting a variety of people and constituencies under high visibility.

☐ International Assignments – requiring communicating to a new and diverse population and making decisions and taking actions with less direct support and supervision.

☐ Staff Leadership (influencing without authority) – acting across organizational boundaries without the power to command attention and compliance.

☐ Start-Ups – requiring forging a new team and acting on a variety of new and first-time subjects on a tight timetable with little precedence.

Part-Time Assignments That Would Add Skills in This Dimension

☐ Manage a group of balky and resisting people through an unpopular change or project.

☐ Take on a tough and undoable project, one where others who have tried it have failed.

☐ Manage a group of people involved in tackling a fix-it or turnaround project.

☐ Help shut down a plant, regional office, product line, business, operation, etc.

☐ Handle a tough negotiation with an internal or external client or customer, or manage a dissatisfied internal or external customer; troubleshoot a performance or quality problem with a product or service.

☐ Resolve an issue in conflict between two people, units, geographies, functions, etc.

☐ Make peace with an enemy or someone you've disappointed with a product or service or someone you've had some trouble with or don't get along with very well.

☐ Manage a group through a significant business crisis.

☐ Manage a cost-cutting project where the cuts are deep.

☐ Plan a new site for a building (plant, field office, headquarters, etc.).

22

FACTOR III: CHANGE AGILITY

☐ Work on a team that has to integrate diverse systems (move from using five computer platforms into one), processes (integrating a distinct, stand-alone, quality-assurance process into a product development process), or procedures (five competency models into one) across decentralized and/or dispersed units where you have to find the most common solution.

☐ Plan a first-time off-site meeting, conference, convention, trade show, event, etc.

☐ Prepare and present a proposal of some consequence to top management.

☐ Manage the renovation of an office, floor, building, meeting room, warehouse, etc.

☐ Work on a team that's deciding whom to keep and whom to let go in a layoff, shutdown, delayering, or divestiture.

☐ Be a member of a union-negotiating or grievance-handling team.

☐ Be a change agent; create a symbol for change; lead the rallying cry; champion a significant change and implementation.

There are two ways of meeting difficulties:
You alter the difficulties or you alter yourself to meet them.
Phyllis Bottome – British novelist

22

Suggested Readings

Bolton, R. (1986). *People skills: How to assert yourself, listen to others and resolve conflicts.* New York, NY: Simon & Schuster, Inc.

Furlong, G. T. (2005). *The conflict resolution toolbox: Models and maps for analyzing, diagnosing, and resolving conflict.* Mississauga, ON: John Wiley & Sons Canada Ltd.

George, B. (with Sims, P.). (2007). *True north: Discover your authentic leadership.* San Francisco, CA: Jossey-Bass.

Gerzon, M. (2006). *Leading through conflict: How successful leaders transform differences into opportunities.* Boston, MA: Harvard Business School Press.

Kheel, T. W. (2001). *The keys to conflict resolution: Proven methods of resolving disputes voluntarily.* New York, NY: Four Walls Eight Windows.

Lee, G., & Elliott-Lee, D. (2006). *Courage: The backbone of leadership.* San Francisco, CA: Jossey-Bass.

Levine, S. (2009). *Getting to resolution: Turning conflict into collaboration* (2nd ed.). San Francisco, CA: Berrett-Koehler Publishers.

Maginn, M. D. (2007). *Managing in times of change.* New York, NY: McGraw-Hill.

McConnon, S., & McConnon, M. (2008). *Conflict management in the workplace: How to manage disagreements and develop trust and understanding* (3rd ed.). Oxford, UK: How To Books, Ltd.

Mortensen, K. (2008). *Persuasion IQ: The 10 skills you need to get exactly what you want.* New York, NY: AMACOM.

Runde, C., & Flanagan, T. A. (2006). *Becoming a conflict competent leader: How you and your organization can manage conflict effectively.* San Francisco, CA: Jossey-Bass.

Treasurer, B. (2008). *Courage goes to work: How to build backbones, boost performance, and get results.* San Francisco, CA: Berrett-Koehler Publishers.

Van Slyke, E. J. (1999). *Listening to conflict: Finding constructive solutions to workplace disputes.* New York, NY: AMACOM.

Warrell, M. (2008). *Find your courage: 12 Acts for becoming fearless at work and in life.* New York, NY: McGraw-Hill.

22

FACTOR III: CHANGE AGILITY

22

Dimension 23
Visioning

Good business leaders create a vision, articulate the vision,
passionately own the vision, and relentlessly drive it to completion.
Jack Welch – Former Chairman and CEO of General Electric

Skilled
Introduces a different slant; good at "what ifs" and scenarios.

Unskilled
Doesn't come up with new or many wrinkles to the old; may have trouble seeing fresh scenarios or where they might lead.

Items
- ☐ 23. Asks "Why can't it be done?"
- ☐ 50. Introduces a different slant into almost any discussion.
- ☐ 77. Good at envisioning and playing "what if" games and exercises; good at generating multiple scenarios.

Leadership Architect® Competencies Most Associated with This Dimension

Strong
- ☐ 2. *Dealing with* Ambiguity
- ☐ 14. Creativity
- ☐ 46. Perspective
- ☐ 51. Problem Solving

Moderate
- ☐ 12. Conflict Management
- ☐ 57. Standing Alone
- ☐ 58. Strategic Agility
- ☐ 65. *Managing* Vision and Purpose

Light
- ☐ 28. Innovation Management
- ☐ 30. Intellectual Horsepower
- ☐ 32. Learning on the Fly

23

Some Causes

- ☐ Avoids risks
- ☐ Defensive
- ☐ Doesn't like being first or out front of others
- ☐ Doesn't like to speculate
- ☐ Fear of rejection of ideas
- ☐ Narrow background
- ☐ Not creative
- ☐ Not curious
- ☐ Prefers past solutions
- ☐ Prefers to stick with what is known
- ☐ Shy and withdrawn
- ☐ Single-tracked
- ☐ Too comfortable with what is

Developmental Difficulty

Harder

The Map

Visioning is an acquired skill, a combination of accessing history and trends and thinking ahead. How successful could you be if you knew all of the scores of future athletic contests? What if you knew the outcome of future professional fights? The winner of the World Series? Which stocks will go up in the market? What about the next trend in your business? The next market or country to latch onto your product or service? The next way to organize companies to be more productive? The next big thing in your product line? Visioning opens the door to the future and increases your chances of acting on target when the future gets here. The best way to prepare for an event is to know about it ahead of time. An even better path is to create the future you want.

Some Remedies and Workarounds

- ☐ 1. **Missing context? Know your history.** Futuring is a series of educated "what ifs." To make more informed guesses, read periodicals with a global perspective, such as the *New York Times*, the *Economist*, *International Herald Tribune*, *BusinessWeek*, *Forbes*, *Futurist*, and the *Atlantic*. These periodicals do an excellent job of setting historical context as well as explaining how things got to be the way they are. The more you know about past and present trends, the better your "what ifs" will become.

- ☐ 2. **Focused only on your immediate work? Learn more about your business.** Talk to the people who know. Meet with the strategic planners,

23

and read every significant document you can find about your business, its customers and competitors. Reduce your understanding to rules of thumb and use these to image what initiatives could make a huge difference.

☐ **3. Concrete thinker? Work on your visual side.** Learn storyboarding—a pictorial technique of representing a problem or process. Use mind mapping, a wonderfully branching way to plan, examine ideas, and simply think differently. Get some scenario training, then implement it with your team to come up with likely futures. Use flowcharting software packages. Close your eyes and see what the outcome would look like. Come up with an image or symbol that embodies the vision. People are much more likely to get excited by stories, symbols, and images than a white paper explaining the plan.

☐ **4. Driven by logic? Make your mind a bit sillier.** You don't have to tell anyone what you're doing. Ask what song is this problem like? Find an analogy to your problem in nature, in children's toys, in anything that has a physical structure.

☐ **5. Trouble putting it all together? Look for anomalies, unusual facts that don't quite fit in.** Why did sales go down when they should have gone up? It could be random, but maybe not. Look for patterns, something present in failures but not present in successes. Even more useful, look for elements present in successes but never present in a failure. This will yield some insight into underlying principles.

☐ **6. Not finding solutions in your own organization? Hunt for parallels in other organizations and in remote areas totally outside your field.** By this, we don't mean best practices, which come and go. Find a parallel situation to the underlying issue—for example, who has to do things really fast (Domino's, FedEx)? Who has to deal with maximum ambiguity (emergency room, a newspaper, police dispatchers)?

☐ **7. Stuck in the present? Hunt for parallels in history.** There are always plenty of candidates. Harry Truman used the presidential archives to form what he called his "council of presidents" to see what others had done in parallel situations.

☐ **8. Difficulty venturing beyond tried-and-true solutions? Convene a group with the widest possible variety of backgrounds.** (Yes, we mean widest. It makes no difference if they know anything about the problem.) During World War II, it was discovered that groups with maximum diversity produced the most creative solutions to problems. You're looking for fresh approaches here, not practicality. That comes later as you sift through the ideas.

23

☐ 9. *(Workaround)* **Lacking critical skills? Get reinforcement.** Leave the visioning to others. Hire an expert. Acknowledge its importance and get out of the way. Don't reject ideas too soon. Let them simmer. If you do reject, provide the why. Give them time and resources. Let the creative juices flow. Don't criticize. Don't require outcomes too soon. If you have given up on becoming a visionary, you have to be patient with others and give them leeway and time.

☐ 10. *(Workaround)* **Can't do it all on your own? Share the visioning task with your team.** Get everyone visioning. Be the ringmaster. Let the visions flow without evaluation at first. Then test them for credibility. Narrow them down to the few most likely possibilities. Then draw up an action plan for each of them.

More Help?

In addition to the 10 tips listed for this dimension, there are some tips that may apply from *FYI For Your Improvement*™. We have coded each item to about 10 tips from the *FYI* book. To use this resource, the codes below refer to the chapter and then the tip number from the *FYI* book. For example, in item 23 below, 32-1,2,3,4 refers to Chapter 32 – Learning on the Fly, tips 1,2,3 and 4. If you don't have a copy of *FYI*, it is available through Lominger International at 952-345-3610 or www.lominger.com.

23. Asks "Why can't it be done?"

    32-1,2,3,4; 51-4; 57-1,3,5,7,8

50. Introduces a different slant into almost any discussion.

    14-1,3,4,5; 32-1,2,3; 46-1; 58-3,9

77. Good at envisioning and playing "what if" games and exercises; good at generating multiple scenarios.

    5-6; 14-1,2; 46-1,2,3; 58-3,4,6; 65-9

Jobs That Would Add Skills in This Dimension

☐ Fix-Its/Turnarounds – requiring making tough strategic and tactical decisions impacting a variety of people and constituencies and communicating the vision clearly and quickly.

☐ Heavy Strategic Demands – requiring significant strategic thinking and planning which charts new ground, along with selling the vision to a critical audience.

☐ International Assignments – requiring strategizing in a new environment and communicating the vision to new and different people.

☐ Scope (complexity) Assignments – requiring strategizing on a number of different fronts while tying it all into a single trust and vision message.

☐ Start-Ups – requiring creating a from-the-ground-up strategy and vision to motivate new people on a tight timetable.

Part-Time Assignments That Would Add Skills in This Dimension

☐ Relaunch an existing product or service that's not doing well, requiring a new vision.

☐ Launch a new product, service, or process.

☐ Take on a tough and undoable project, one where others who have tried it have failed where a new approach is needed.

☐ Manage a temporary group of people involved in tackling a fix-it or turnaround project where a new solution is called for.

☐ Prepare and present a strategic proposal of some consequence to top management which involves a change in direction.

☐ Build a multi-functional project team to tackle a common business issue or problem.

☐ Work on a team that has to integrate diverse systems (move from using five computer platforms into one), processes (integrating a distinct, stand-alone, quality-assurance process into a product development process), or procedures (five competency models into one) across decentralized and/or dispersed units where you have to find the most common solution.

☐ Work on a project that involves travel and study of an issue, acquisition, or joint venture off-shore or overseas, and report back to management.

☐ Manage a group through a significant business crisis.

☐ Seek out and use a seed budget to create and pursue a personal idea, product, or service.

Obstacles are those frightful things you see
when you take your eyes off your goal.
Henry Ford – Founder of Ford Motor Company

23

147

Suggested Readings

Adair, J. (2005). *The inspirational leader: How to motivate, encourage and achieve success.* Philadelphia: Kogan Page.

Atlantic. http://www.theatlantic.com.

Bates, S. (2008). *Motivate like a CEO: Communicate your strategic vision and inspire people to act!* New York, NY: McGraw-Hill.

BusinessWeek. http://www.businessweek.com.

Center for Creative Leadership, Cartwright, T., & Baldwin, D. (2007). *Communicating your vision.* Hoboken, NJ: Pfeiffer.

Champy, J., Nohria, N. (2001). *The arc of ambition: Defining the leadership journey.* New York, NY: John Wiley & Sons.

Collins, J. (2001). *Good to great.* New York, NY: Harper Collins.

Commentary Magazine. http://www.commentarymagazine.com.

De Bono, E. (1999). *Six thinking hats* (2nd ed.). Boston, MA: Little, Brown and Co.

Drucker, P. (2001). *Management challenges for the 21st century.* New York, NY: HarperBusiness.

Dudik, E. (2000). *Strategic renaissance: New thinking and innovative tools to create great corporate strategies: Using insights from history and science.* New York, NY: AMACOM.

Economist. http://www.economist.com.

Futurist Magazine. http://www.wfs.org.

Hamel, G. (2002). *Leading the revolution: How to thrive in turbulent times by making innovation a way of life.* Boston, MA: Harvard Business School Press.

Hamel, G., & Prahalad, C. K. (1996). *Competing for the future.* Boston, MA: Harvard Business School Press.

International Herald Tribune. http://www.iht.com.

Kanter, R. M., Kao, J., & Wiersema, F. (Eds.). (1997). *Innovation: Breakthrough thinking at 3M, DuPont, GE, Pfizer and Rubbermaid.* New York, NY: HarperCollins Publishers.

Kennedy, P. M. (1987). *The rise and fall of the great powers: Economic change and military conflict from 1500 to 2000.* New York, NY: Random House.

Kotter, J. P. (1996). *Leading change.* Boston, MA: Harvard Business School Press.

Kotter, J. P. (2008). *A sense of urgency.* Boston, MA: Harvard Business Press.

Kotter, J. P., & Cohen, D. S. (2002). *The heart of change: Real-life stories of how people change their organizations.* Boston, MA: Harvard Business School Press.

Kouzes, J. M., & Posner, B. Z. (2007). *The leadership challenge* (4th ed.). San Francisco, CA: Jossey-Bass.

Kumar, S., & Whitefield, F. (2008). *Visionaries: The 20th century's 100 most inspirational leaders.* White River Junction, VT: Chelsea Green Publishing.

Lasley, M. (2004). *Courageous visions: How to unleash passionate energy in your life and your organization.* Burlington, PA: Discovery Press.

Ogilvy, J. A. (2002). *Creating better futures: Scenario planning as a tool for a better tomorrow.* New York, NY: Oxford University Press.

Ringland, G. (2006). *Scenario planning: Managing for the future* (2nd ed.). West Sussex, England: John Wiley & Sons Ltd.

Van der Heijden, K. (2005). *Scenarios: The art of strategic conversion* (2nd ed.). West Sussex, England: John Wiley & Sons Ltd.

Wall Street Journal. http://www.wsj.com.

23

FACTOR III: CHANGE AGILITY

23

Factor IV
Results Agility

High
This Factor measures various components of delivering results under first-time or tough situations. People high on this Factor pull things off under difficult conditions and build high-performing teams. They do so partially by personal drive and adaptability.

Low
People low on this Factor have more trouble with first-time or difficult situations. They may have problems inspiring others or lack personal drive or presence. Perhaps as a consequence, results suffer when something new is needed.

Some Causes
- ☐ Does the minimum to get by
- ☐ Doesn't like to lead or to be out front alone
- ☐ Flat personality
- ☐ Gets easily upset
- ☐ Lacks intensity and edge
- ☐ Last to try what's new
- ☐ Not ambitious
- ☐ Not comfortable with uncertainty and ambiguity
- ☐ Not resourceful
- ☐ Not well networked
- ☐ Too comfortable with what is

IV

IV

Dimension 24
Inspires Others

If your actions inspire others to dream more, learn more,
do more and become more, you are a leader.
John Q. Adams – 6th President of the United States

Skilled
Can build a team through motivation and through the confidence the team has in him/her.

Unskilled
Has problems with team building; may lack take-charge skills, not be very motivating or fail to build confidence in others.

Items
- [ ] 24. Can inspire a team to work hard.
- [ ] 51. Can state his/her case or viewpoint with energizing passion.
- [ ] 78. Can build and manage a high-performing team.

Leadership Architect® Competencies Most Associated with This Dimension

Strong
- [ ] 9. Command Skills
- [ ] 36. Motivating Others
- [ ] 39. Organizing
- [ ] 60. *Building Effective* Teams
- [ ] 65. *Managing* Vision and Purpose

Moderate
- [ ] 20. Directing Others
- [ ] 27. Informing
- [ ] 35. Managing and Measuring Work
- [ ] 56. Sizing Up People

24

Light

- ☐ 18. Delegation
- ☐ 21. *Managing* Diversity
- ☐ 29. Integrity and Trust
- ☐ 33. Listening
- ☐ 49. Presentation Skills

Some Causes

- ☐ A loner
- ☐ Doesn't like to lead or be out front alone
- ☐ Doesn't listen
- ☐ Doesn't set standards or goals high enough
- ☐ Isn't motivated by winning
- ☐ Not a good role model for hard work
- ☐ Not achievement oriented
- ☐ Not approachable
- ☐ Not creative
- ☐ Not inspirational
- ☐ Not trustworthy
- ☐ Poor communicator
- ☐ Shy or withdrawn
- ☐ Too critical

Developmental Difficulty

Easier

The Map

Much more can be accomplished through others than by oneself. In our years of collecting data on managers and executives, individual skills are typically high, while team skills languish. Getting things done through others is key to success as a manager. Setting goals. Delegating. Measuring. Helping. Correcting. Urging. Rewarding. Celebrating. That's the cycle of inspiration.

Some Remedies and Workarounds

- ☐ 1. **Employees disengaged? Follow the rules of inspiring others.** Communicate importance, celebrate wins, give people ways to measure themselves and see progress, set goals, provide autonomy, provide a variety of tasks. These are the proven winners to get people engaged in their work.

- ☐ 2. **Uncertain how to motivate? Play the motivation odds.** The top motivators at work (unchanged during the past quarter century) are: job

24

challenge, accomplishing something worthwhile, learning new things, personal development, and autonomy. Pay, friendliness, praise, and chance of promotion don't make the top 10.

☐ **3. Lacking team cohesiveness? Establish common cause.** Nothing galvanizes people like a shared purpose, which is what holds any group together. Get everyone involved in sharing a common vision. Don't leave out the quiet or the reluctant. Repeatedly sell the logic of pulling together, listen, ask questions, invite suggestions to reach the outcome. Leave how things are to be done as open as possible. Specified sequences can be demotivating, even boring. People work harder under conditions of choice. Encourage experimentation.

☐ **4. Don't believe in teams? Talk to the believers.** You're probably a strong individual achiever who doesn't like the mess and time expenditure of team processes. To change your thinking, observe and talk with three excellent team builders and ask them why they manage this way. Chances are they are not that different from you, as team building is not a common skill. Learn from others who probably had the same doubts that you do now.

☐ **5. Don't know how to build a team? Know the building blocks of great teams.** Here are five characteristics of high-performance teams:
  – They have a shared mind-set.
  – They trust one another—cover for each other, pitch in, are candid, deal with issues directly.
  – They have the talent collectively to do the job.
  – They operate efficiently, doing the small things well—running meetings, assigning work, dealing with conflict.
  – Most central to their excellence, they focus outside the team on customers and results. They do not focus much internally on atmosphere and happiness. This, however, is a characteristic of low-performing teams, who tend to delude themselves about their performance and focus on harmony.

☐ **6. Fixing others' problems for them? Be a teacher.** Always explain your thinking. Work out loud with them on a task. What do you see as important? How do you know? What questions are you asking? What steps are you following? Simply firing out solutions will make people more dependent at best.

☐ **7. Inexperienced team? Learn how to develop others.** Developing direct reports and others is dead last in skill level among the 67 competencies of the Leadership Architect® and has been since we started collecting these data. To develop people, you have to follow the essential rules of

24

155

development. They take a bit of time. Development is not simply sending someone to a course:

- Start with a portrait of the person's strengths and weaknesses. They can't grow if they are misinformed about themselves.
- Provide ongoing feedback from multiple sources.
- Give them progressively stretching tasks that are first-time and different for them. At least 70% of reported development occurs through challenging assignments that demand skill development. People don't grow from doing more of the same.
- Encourage them to think of themselves as learners, not just accomplishers. What are they learning that is new or different? What skills have grown in the last year? What have they learned that they can use in other situations?
- Use coursework, books, development partners, and mentoring to reinforce learning.

☐ **8. Concrete thinker? Work on your visual side.** Learn storyboarding—a pictorial technique of representing a problem or process. Use mind mapping, a wonderfully branching way to plan, examine ideas, and simply think differently. Get some scenario training, then implement it with your team to come up with likely futures. Use flowcharting software packages. Close your eyes and see what the outcome would look like. Come up with an image or symbol that embodies the vision. People are much more likely to get excited by stories, symbols, and images than a white paper explaining the plan.

☐ **9. *(Workaround)* Lacking critical skills? Get reinforcement.** Delegate inspiration to your team. If you aren't going to do it, give them a chance. Be more participative than the natural you. Get them involved in everything the team does. Let them set goals and agree how to measure them. Let them do the measurement and determine the rewards. Let them celebrate. You can get out of being more inspirational yourself if you let others get totally involved.

☐ **10. *(Workaround)* Not enough time? Use your network.** Engage an internal or external coach to help you determine what to do. Use someone who is good at determining the best way to approach people and knows how to motivate and inspire others. In time, some may rub off, but the important goal is to begin doing what needs to be done.

24

More Help?

In addition to the 10 tips listed for this dimension, there are some tips that may apply from *FYI For Your Improvement*™. We have coded each item to about 10 tips from the *FYI* book. To use this resource, the codes below refer to the chapter and then the tip number from the *FYI* book. For example, in item 24 below, 36-1,2,3 refers to Chapter 36 – Motivating Others, tips 1,2 and 3. If you don't have a copy of *FYI*, it is available through Lominger International at 952-345-3610 or www.lominger.com.

24. Can inspire a team to work hard.

   36-1,2,3; 60-1,4,6; 110-1,2,4,9

51. Can state his/her case or viewpoint with energizing passion.

   1-6; 49-2,4; 57-9; 65-1,2,5,6; 67-4,7

78. Can build and manage a high-performing team.

   18-1; 19-1; 35-7; 36-1; 60-1,4,6; 110-1,2,4

Jobs That Would Add Skills in This Dimension

☐ Fix-Its/Turnarounds – requiring making tough decisions impacting a variety of people and constituencies in a negative environment.

☐ Scale (size shift) Assignments – managing larger numbers of people, most of them remote and several layers deep.

☐ Scope (complexity) Assignments – requiring managing a variety of people from different functions and activities about a variety of topics.

☐ Significant People Demands – requiring managing a large number of people, usually in dispersed structures.

☐ Staff Leadership (influencing without authority) – working across organizational boundaries without the positional power to command attention and compliance.

☐ Start-Ups – requiring forging a new team and initiating a variety of new and first-time initiatives on a tight timetable.

Part-Time Assignments That Would Add Skills in This Dimension

☐ Manage a group of balky and resisting people through an unpopular change or project.

☐ Assemble a team of diverse people to accomplish a difficult task.

☐ Build a multi-functional or multi-divisional project team to tackle a common business issue or problem.

☐ Manage a group of people involved in tackling a fix-it or turnaround project.

24

□ Manage a group of "green," inexperienced people as their coach, teacher, guide, etc.

□ Relaunch an existing product or service that's not doing well.

□ Manage a group of people who are older and/or more experienced to accomplish a task.

□ Manage a group of low-competence people through a task they couldn't do by themselves.

□ Manage a group including former peers to accomplish a task.

□ Be a change agent; create a symbol for change; lead the rallying cry; champion a significant change and implementation.

□ Create employee involvement teams.

□ Manage a group through a significant business crisis.

Start with good people, lay out the rules, communicate with your employees, motivate them and reward them. If you do all those things effectively, you can't miss.
Lee Iacocca – Former Chairman and CEO of Chrysler Corporation

24

Suggested Readings

Adair, J. (2005). *The inspirational leader: How to motivate, encourage and achieve success.* Philadelphia: Kogan Page.

Autry, J. A. (2004). *The servant leader: How to build a creative team, develop great morale, and improve bottom-line performance.* New York, NY: Three River Press.

Bolton, R. (1986). *People skills: How to assert yourself, listen to others and resolve conflicts.* New York, NY: Simon & Schuster, Inc.

Daniels, A. C. (2000). *Bringing out the best in people: How to apply the astonishing power of positive reinforcement* (2nd ed.). New York, NY: McGraw-Hill.

Deeprose, D. (2006). *How to recognize and reward employees: 150 Ways to inspire peak performance* (2nd ed.). New York, NY: AMACOM.

Gostick, A., & Elton, C. (2007). *The carrot principle: How the best managers use recognition to engage their employees, retain talent, and drive performance.* New York, NY: Free Press.

Harvard Business School Press (2005). *Motivating people for improved performance.* Boston, MA: Harvard Business School Press.

Hiam, A. (2003). *Motivational management: Inspiring your people for maximum performance.* New York, NY: AMACOM.

Katzenbach, J. R., & Smith, D. K. (2003). *The wisdom of teams: Creating the high-performance organization.* New York, NY: HarperBusiness.

Kaye, B., & Jordan-Evans, S. (2008). *Love 'em or lose 'em: Getting good people to stay* (4th ed.). San Francisco, CA: Berrett-Koehler Publishers.

Kouzes, J. M., & Posner, B. Z. (2003). *Encouraging the heart: A leader's guide to rewarding and recognizing others.* San Francisco, CA: Jossey-Bass.

Mitroff, I.I. (with Anagnos, G.). (2001). *Managing crises before they happen: What every executive and manager needs to know about crisis management.* New York, NY: AMACOM.

Podmoroff, D. (2005). *365 Ways to motivate and reward your employees every day: With little or no money.* Ocala, FL: Atlantic Publishing Group.

Robbins, H., & Finley, M. (2000). *The new why teams don't work: What goes wrong and how to make it right.* San Francisco, CA: Berrett-Koehler Publishers.

24

FACTOR IV: RESULTS AGILITY

Ruyle, K. E., Eichinger, R. W., & De Meuse, K. P. (2009). *FYI for talent engagement: Drivers of best practice for managers and business leaders.* Minneapolis, MN: Lominger International: A Korn/Ferry Company.

Sirota, D., Mischkind, L. A., & Meltzer, M. I. (2005). *The enthusiastic employee: How companies profit by giving workers what they want.* Upper Saddle River, NJ: Wharton School Publishing.

24

Dimension 25
Delivers Results

To achieve great things, two things are needed:
a plan, and not quite enough time.
Leonard Bernstein – American conductor, composer, and pianist

Skilled
Performs well under first-time, changing or tough conditions.

Unskilled
Has problems with the new, unusual or the changing. Results may suffer.

Items
- ☐ 25. Performs well under first-time conditions; isn't thrown by changing circumstances.
- ☐ 52. Has often pulled off things with limited resources.
- ☐ 79. Performs well in tough situations; can be counted on.

Leadership Architect® Competencies Most Associated with This Dimension

Strong
- ☐ 9. Command Skills
- ☐ 39. Organizing
- ☐ 53. *Drive for* Results

Moderate
- ☐ 20. Directing Others
- ☐ 32. Learning on the Fly
- ☐ 51. Problem Solving
- ☐ 57. Standing Alone

Light
- ☐ 1. Action Oriented
- ☐ 16. *Timely* Decision Making
- ☐ 43. Perseverance
- ☐ 50. Priority Setting
- ☐ 52. Process Management

25

Some Causes

☐ Avoids conflict
☐ Defensive
☐ Doesn't like to be first
☐ Gets upset easily
☐ Lazy
☐ Not ambitious
☐ Not resourceful
☐ Prefers past and proven solutions
☐ Slows down when things get tough
☐ Uncomfortable with uncertainty

Developmental Difficulty

Easier

The Map

After all is said and done, results are what count.

Some Remedies and Workarounds

☐ 1. **Clinging to previous solutions? Use mental rehearsal for tough situations.** Learn to recognize the clues that you're about to fall back on old behavior and be ready with a fresh strategy that you have decided in advance. If you know, for example, that a solution isn't working and you're likely to be questioned about it, be ready to engage others and get the benefit of their thinking.

☐ 2. **Wary of criticism? Prepare in advance.** Leading in first-time situations is risky. You have to defend what you're doing, so convince yourself first that you are on the right track. Be prepared to explain again and again, to attract lightning bolts from detractors, from those unsettled by change and from those who will always say it could have been done differently, better, and cheaper. To prepare for this, think about the 10 objections that will come up and mentally rehearse how you will reply. Listen patiently to people's concerns, acknowledge them, then explain why you think the change will be beneficial. Attack positions, but not people.

☐ 3. **Uncertain? Define the problem—don't put it in a familiar box so you can feel comfortable.** What is it and what isn't it? How many causes can you think of? Are you stating things as facts that are really your opinion? Are you generalizing from an example or two? Use patterns and themes to define problems.

☐ 4. **Easily frustrated? Don't expect to get it right the first time.** If a situation is ambiguous, be incremental. Make some small decisions, get

25

instant feedback, treat mistakes and failures as ways to learn. Focus on your third or fourth try, not the first.

☐ **5. Unfamiliar problem? Learn on the fly.** First-time and tough situations call for resourcefulness. First-time means you haven't done exactly this before. So first, define what it is that needs to be done. Then set final and progress goals and measures. Next, try to lay out the work in incremental steps with the full expectation that this will change and evolve over time. Then find and bargain for the resources you will need to perform. Get the support you need and rally the team that will be working on the project. Delegate as much as possible. Celebrate incremental gains. Experiment and expect some false paths and mistakes. Have a process for instant correction of the plan. Make things up on the fly. Expect the unexpected. All the while, relentlessly drive toward the original goals.

☐ **6. Losing your composure? Recognize your frustration and anxiety triggers.** Initial anxious responses last 45 to 60 seconds. They are marked by your characteristic emotional response. Learn to recognize your triggers (raising your volume, drumming your fingers, shifting in your chair, etc.). Once you have figured out your triggers, ask why. Is it ego? Extra work? People you dislike or think are lazy? For each grouping, figure out what would be a more mature response. Learn to delay your response. Count to 10 or ask a clarifying question. Stall until the initial burst of glucose and adrenaline subsides.

☐ **7. Trouble shifting gears? Study your daily transition points.** It's all in a day's work: going from a tense meeting to a celebration for a notable accomplishment. Think of your day as a series of transitions. For a week, monitor your gear-shifting behavior at work and at home. What transitions give you the most trouble? The least? Why? Practice gear-shifting transitions. On the way between activities, think about the transition you're making and the frame of mind required to make it.

☐ **8. Give up too soon on an idea? Try different approaches.** If you have trouble going back the second or third time, then switch approaches. For example, you could meet with all stakeholders, a single key stakeholder, present the idea to a group, call in an expert to buttress your innovation, or project various scenarios showing the value of the idea.

☐ **9. Have trouble getting it done across boundaries? Start bargaining.** Don't just ask for things; find some common ground where you can provide help. What do your peers and other essential stakeholders need? If it affects them negatively, you can appeal to the common good, trade something, or figure out some way to minimize the impact. Go into these relationships with a trading mentality, not a handout mentality.

25

☐ **10.** *(Workaround)* Not looking for challenges? Stay out of first-time situations. If you are content to be you and not perform well in new and different situations, keep yourself out of them. Play with the cards you have. Turn down jobs and assignments that involve fresh challenges. Concentrate on being a very strong performer in the areas you are comfortable in. Work on your functional expertise. Specialize doing a little better tomorrow what you do well today. Leave cutting a path through the jungle to others more bold and adventurous.

More Help?

In addition to the 10 tips listed for this dimension, there are some tips that may apply from *FYI For Your Improvement*™. We have coded each item to about 10 tips from the *FYI* book. To use this resource, the codes below refer to the chapter and then the tip number from the *FYI* book. For example, in item 25 below, 2-1,2,4,5,7 refers to Chapter 2 – *Dealing with* Ambiguity, tips 1,2,4,5 and 7. If you don't have a copy of *FYI*, it is available through Lominger International at 952-345-3610 or www.lominger.com.

25. Performs well under first-time conditions; isn't thrown by changing circumstances.

   2-1,2,4,5,7; 32-1,4,9; 40-1; 51-5

52. Has often pulled off things with limited resources.

   53-1,2,3,4,5,6,7,8,9,10

79. Performs well in tough situations; can be counted on.

   9-1,2,3,4,5,10; 12-7; 13-2; 40-9; 53-1

Jobs That Would Add Skills in This Dimension

☐ Chair of Projects/Task Forces – requiring finding new and effective solutions under tight deadlines and high visibility on an issue that matters to people higher up.

☐ Fix-Its/Turnarounds – requiring making things happen on a tight schedule that are new and different in a negative environment.

☐ Scale (size shift) Assignments – managing larger numbers of people and being responsible for significant outcomes.

☐ Scope (complexity) Assignments – requiring getting things done across diverse units.

25

☐ Staff Leadership (influencing without authority) – getting things done across organizational boundaries without the power to command attention and compliance.

☐ Start-Ups – requiring forging a new team and acting on several simultaneous fronts with few precedents to go on.

Part-Time Assignments That Would Add Skills in This Dimension

☐ Manage a group of people involved in tackling a fix-it or turnaround project.

☐ Relaunch an existing product or service that's not doing well.

☐ Manage a group of balky and resisting people through an unpopular change or project.

☐ Help shut down a plant, regional office, product line, business, operation, etc.

☐ Manage a group through a significant business crisis.

☐ Assemble a team of diverse people to accomplish a difficult task.

☐ Launch a new product, service, or process.

☐ Manage a group of people in a rapidly expanding operation.

☐ Build a multi-functional project team to tackle a common business issue or problem.

☐ Take on a tough and undoable project, one where others who have tried it have failed.

☐ Manage a group of low-competence people through a task they couldn't do by themselves.

☐ Manage the renovation of an office, floor, building, meeting room, warehouse, etc.

☐ Plan for and start up something small (secretarial pool, athletic program, suggestion system, program, etc.).

☐ Integrate diverse systems, processes, or procedures across decentralized and/or dispersed units.

☐ Manage a deep cost-cutting project.

Because a thing seems difficult for you,
do not think it impossible for anyone to accomplish.
Marcus Aurelius (121 CE - 180 CE) – Roman emperor and philosopher

25

Suggested Readings

Austin, J. (2006). *What no one ever tells you about leading for results: Best practices from 101 real-world leaders.* Chicago: Kaplan Business.

Baldoni, J. (2006). *How great leaders get great results.* New York, NY: McGraw-Hill.

Bolton, R. (1986). *People skills: How to assert yourself, listen to others and resolve conflicts.* New York, NY: Simon & Schuster, Inc.

Bossidy, L., & Charan, R. (with Burck, C.). (2002). *Execution: The discipline of getting things done.* New York, NY: Crown Business.

Drucker, P. F. (2006). *Managing for results.* New York, NY: HarperCollins.

Duke Corporate Education. (2005). *Influencing and collaborating for results.* Chicago: Kaplan Business.

Kaplan, R. S., & Norton, D. P. (2008). *The execution premium: Linking strategy to operations for competitive advantage.* Boston, MA: Harvard Business School Press.

Kendrick, T. (2006). *Results without authority: Controlling a project when the team doesn't report to you.* New York, NY: AMACOM.

Kheel, T. W. (2001). *The keys to conflict resolution: Proven methods of resolving disputes voluntarily.* New York, NY: Four Walls Eight Windows.

Kotter, J. P., & Cohen, D. S. (2002). *The heart of change: Real-life stories of how people change their organizations.* Boston, MA: Harvard Business School Press.

Lefton, R. E., & Loeb, J. T. (2004). *Why can't we get anything done around here? The smart manager's guide to executing the work that delivers results.* New York, NY: McGraw-Hill.

Studer, Q. (2008). *Results that last: Hardwiring behaviors that will take your company to the top.* Hoboken, NJ: John Wiley & Sons.

Van Slyke, E. J. (1999). *Listening to conflict: Finding constructive solutions to workplace disputes.* New York, NY: AMACOM.

Dimension 26
Drive

History has demonstrated that the most notable winners
usually encountered heartbreaking obstacles before they triumphed.
They won because they refused to become discouraged by their defeats.
B. C. Forbes – Scottish-born financial journalist
and founder of *Forbes* magazine

Skilled
Works hard on many fronts; high standards of excellence.

Unskilled
May have difficulty with many balls in the air at once; may not be willing to make personal sacrifices, or may have lower standards of excellence than needed.

Items
- ☐ 26. Can work on many things at once; is a multi-track person.
- ☐ 53. Is willing to work hard and make personal sacrifices to get ahead.
- ☐ 80. Has high internal standards of excellence in addition to being tuned to outside standards.

Leadership Architect® Competencies Most Associated with This Dimension

Strong
- ☐ 1. Action Oriented
- ☐ 43. Perseverance
- ☐ 53. *Drive for* Results

Moderate
- ☐ 6. Career Ambition
- ☐ 32. Learning on the Fly
- ☐ 50. Priority Setting
- ☐ 57. Standing Alone

26

Light

- ☐ 2. *Dealing with* Ambiguity
- ☐ 16. *Timely* Decision Making
- ☐ 35. Managing and Measuring Work

Some Causes

- ☐ Does the minimum to get by
- ☐ Has low standards
- ☐ Isn't inspired by winning
- ☐ Isn't motivated by what is done at work
- ☐ Lazy
- ☐ Lives in a comfort zone
- ☐ Not ambitious
- ☐ Puts a high value on balance between work and personal life
- ☐ Self-centered and selfish
- ☐ Single-tracked
- ☐ Tires easily

Developmental Difficulty

Easier

The Map

Drive and inspiration make the world go around. Finding the passion to perform is one key to success and accomplishment. Anyone will work harder when they are working on something they are passionate about. Besides personal passion, it is the role of the manager and leader to help others find their passion. And in some cases, to create passion where none existed before. Passion eases the difficulty of working on several things at once. It adds persistence.

Some Remedies and Workarounds

- ☐ 1. **Lost your passion for the job? Focus on your interests.** Make a list of what you like to do and don't like to do. Concentrate on doing a few things you like each day. See if you can delegate or trade for more desirable activities. Do your least-preferred activities first. Focus not on the activity but on your sense of accomplishment. Volunteer for task forces and projects that would be more interesting for you.

- ☐ 2. **Not taking risks? Get out of your comfort zone.** Find an activity that goes against your natural likes and try it. Up your risk comfort. Start small so you can recover quickly. Pick a few smaller tasks or challenges and build the skill bit by bit. For example, if strategy is your area, write a strategic plan for your unit and show it to people to get feedback, then write a second draft. Devise a strategy for turning one of your hobbies (i.e., photography) into a business.

☐ **3. Unwilling to make sacrifices? Take on a tough assignment.** Many people turn down career opportunities based upon current life comforts, only to regret it later when they are passed by. Perhaps you love what you do now and can't imagine doing anything else. The problem with that is needs change, and if you don't, your prospects are not bright. That scary and unappealing new job will add new skills and variety to your resume at the least. Most successful people have taken any number of jobs which didn't appeal but which did broaden them.

☐ **4. Bought into myths? Learn the facts about success.** Perhaps you don't know how successful careers are really built. What has staying power is performing in a variety of jobs, not more of the same jobs, having a few notable strengths, and seeking new tasks that you don't know how to do. A successful career is built on stress and newness. Talk to some successful people in your organization and hear how random their careers likely have been. Read *The Lessons of Experience* (McCall, Lombardo, & Morrison, 1988), *High Flyers* (McCall, 1998), and *Breaking the Glass Ceiling* (Morrison, White, & VanVelsor, 1994) to see how successful executives grew over time.

☐ **5. Playing it safe? Take more risks.** Research indicates that more successful people have made more mistakes than the less successful. You can't learn anything if you're not trying anything new. Start small, experiment a bit. Go for small wins so you can recover quickly if you miss and, more important, learn from the results. Start with the easiest challenge, then work up to the tougher ones.

☐ **6. Lost your focus? Revisit your priorities.** Some people get results but don't focus on the most important priorities. Successful managers typically spend half their time on two or three key priorities. They don't flit from task to task, working on whatever comes up. They give attention, but not too much, to lesser priorities. The key questions are: What should you be spending half your time on? Can you name five priorities that are less critical than these? If you can't, then you are not differentiating well.

☐ **7. Frustrated easily? Don't try to get it right the first time.** If a situation is ambiguous, be incremental. Make some small decisions, get instant feedback, treat mistakes and failures as ways to learn. Focus on your third or fourth try, not the first.

☐ **8. Doing it all yourself? Delegate, delegate, delegate.** Why aren't you delegating? Are you a perfectionist, wanting everything to be just so?

26

Unrealistic expectations? Won't risk giving out tough work? If this is you, expect career trouble. Better managers delegate more and work shorter hours than managers who try to control most things. The keys are setting priorities, providing help, and designing workflows, not your personal effort. Communicate, set time frames and goals, and get out of the way. Be very clear on what and when, be very open on how. People are more motivated when they can determine the how themselves. Encourage them to try things. Delegate complete tasks, not pieces. Allow more time than it would take you to do it.

☐ **9. Difficulty sustaining momentum? Create powerful goals.** Use goals for yourself and others to build passion and drive. Almost everyone is motivated by achieving goals. Especially if they have had a hand in setting them. Make goals small and reasonably achievable. Set incremental goals or process goals. Don't just set the outcome or end goals. Create a goal process so there can be a lot of celebrating along the way.

☐ **10. *(Workaround)* Not motivated to work harder? Leverage technology and others' skills.** If you don't want to work harder, work smarter. Learn the technologies of work process design. Study things like TQM, process engineering, and Six Sigma. Use tools that make designing and managing work easier. Get it right the first time so you don't have to do rework. Hire the best people and delegate. Look for the easier assignments that still fit into your career path. Work for good companies and good bosses so there is less noise and distraction. Compromise on pay and promotions. If you chose to lay back and not push performance to the higher levels, your rewards will be less and your promotions less frequent.

More Help?

In addition to the 10 tips listed for this dimension, there are some tips that may apply from *FYI For Your Improvement*™. We have coded each item to about 10 tips from the *FYI* book. To use this resource, the codes below refer to the chapter and then the tip number from the *FYI* book. For example, in item 26 below, 2-1,2,3,4,10 refers to Chapter 2 – *Dealing with* Ambiguity, tips 1,2,3,4 and 10. If you don't have a copy of *FYI*, it is available through Lominger International at 952-345-3610 or www.lominger.com.

26. Can work on many things at once; is a multi-track person.
    2-1,2,3,4,10; 18-1; 40-1,9; 50-2,3

53. Is willing to work hard and make personal sacrifices to get ahead.
    1-6,10; 6-1,3,8; 9-1,9,10; 118-7,8

80. Has high internal standards of excellence in addition to being tuned to outside standards.
    1-6,10; 6-3,5,8; 57-8; 101-2,3,6; 118-1

26

Jobs That Would Add Skills in This Dimension

☐ Chair of Projects/Task Forces – requiring finding new and effective solutions under tight deadlines and high visibility on an issue that matters to people higher up.

☐ Fix-Its/Turnarounds – requiring making tough decisions impacting a variety of people and constituencies in a tough environment under negative conditions.

☐ International Assignments – requiring getting things done on your own with less direct support from headquarters.

☐ Staff Leadership (influencing without authority) – communicating across organizational boundaries without the positional power to command attention and compliance.

☐ Staff to Line Shifts – involving moving from a staff role to a line job where there is a more easily determined bottom line or direct measurement of results.

☐ Start-Ups – requiring forging a new team and initiating a number of simultaneous actions with little guidance from the past under a tight time frame.

Part-Time Assignments That Would Add Skills in This Dimension

☐ Manage a group of people involved in tackling a fix-it or turnaround project.

☐ Manage a group of balky and resisting people through an unpopular change or project.

☐ Relaunch an existing product or service that's not doing well.

☐ Take on a tough and undoable project, one where others who have tried it have failed.

☐ Plan a new site for a building (plant, field office, headquarters, etc.).

☐ Manage the renovation of an office, floor, building, meeting room, warehouse, etc.

☐ Launch a new product, service, or process.

☐ Manage a group of people in a rapidly expanding operation.

☐ Assemble a team of diverse people to accomplish a difficult task.

☐ Manage a group through a significant business crisis.

☐ Plan for and start up something small (secretarial pool, athletic program, suggestion system, program, etc.).

☐ Build a multi-functional project team to tackle a common business issue or problem.

☐ Take on a task you dislike or hate to do.

26

☐ Plan a major new off-site meeting, conference, convention, trade show, event, etc.

☐ Manage a dissatisfied internal or external customer; troubleshoot a performance or quality problem with a product or service.

Energy and persistence conquer all things.
Benjamin Franklin – American scientist, inventor, and author

Suggested Readings

Bossidy, L., & Charan, R. (with Burck, C.). (2002). *Execution: The discipline of getting things done.* New York, NY: Crown Business.

Bryant, T. (2004). *Self-discipline in 10 days: How to go from thinking to doing.* Seattle, WA: HUB Publishing.

Champy, J., & Nohria, N. (2001). *The arc of ambition: Defining the leadership journey.* New York, NY: John Wiley & Sons.

Chandler, S. (2004). *100 Ways to motivate yourself: Change your life forever.* Franklin Lakes, NJ: Career Press.

Christian, K. (2004). *You own worst enemy: Breaking the habit of adult underachievement.* New York, NY: Regan Books.

Loehr, J., & Schwartz, T. (2004). *The power of full engagement: Managing energy, not time, is the key to high performance and personal renewal.* New York, NY: Free Press.

Lombardo, M. M., & Eichinger, R. W. (2004). *The leadership machine.* Minneapolis, MN: Lominger International: A Korn/Ferry Company.

Lowe, T., & Giuliani, R. (2009). *Get motivated! Overcome any obstacle, achieve any goal and accelerate your success with motivational DNA.* New York, NY: Doubleday Publishing.

McCall, M. W., Jr. (1998). *High flyers: Developing the next generation of leaders.* Boston, MA: Harvard Business School Press.

McCall, M. W., Jr., Lombardo, M. M., & Morrison, A. M. (1988). *The lessons of experience: How successful executives develop on the job.* Lexington, MA: Lexington Books.

Morrison, A., White, R., & VanVelsor, E. (1994). *Breaking the glass ceiling: Can women reach the top of America's largest corporations?* (2nd ed.). New York, NY: Basic Books.

Orlick, T. (2007). *In pursuit of excellence* (4th ed.). Champaign, IL: Human Kinetics Publishers.

Schatzkin, P. (2004). *The boy who invented television: A story of inspiration, persistence, and quiet passion.* Terre Haute, IN: Tanglewood Books.

26

Dimension 27
Presence

You don't have to be a "person of influence" to be influential.
In fact, the most influential people in my life
are probably not even aware of the things they've taught me.
Scott Adams – American cartoonist and creator of the *Dilbert* comic strip

Skilled
You know he/she is around; self-assured, can be passionate about beliefs.

Unskilled
May not show or lacks self-confidence; may be reluctant to step forth, or be seen as low-key.

Items
- ☐ 27. People feel more confident when this person is in charge.
- ☐ 54. Exudes self-confidence.
- ☐ 81. Has a significant, noticeable presence.

Leadership Architect® Competencies Most Associated with This Dimension

Strong
- ☐ 9. Command Skills
- ☐ 49. Presentation Skills
- ☐ 57. Standing Alone

Moderate
- ☐ 20. Directing Others
- ☐ 31. Interpersonal Savvy
- ☐ 36. Motivating Others
- ☐ 39. Organizing
- ☐ 65. *Managing* Vision and Purpose

27

Light

- ☐ 11. Composure
- ☐ 12. Conflict Management
- ☐ 16. *Timely* Decision Making
- ☐ 34. Managerial Courage
- ☐ 53. *Drive for* Results

Some Causes

- ☐ A loner
- ☐ Cold and impassionate
- ☐ Flat style
- ☐ Lacks edge
- ☐ No leadership experience or background
- ☐ Not engaging
- ☐ Not self-confident
- ☐ Poor communicator
- ☐ Stays in the background
- ☐ Withdrawn and quiet

Developmental Difficulty

Easier

The Map

If you want to lead, you have to act the part. Lack of confidence, inability to handle push back, and hanging back don't project the presence necessary to lead change. People need to know you are around and what you stand for. Presence creates receptivity in others. They will stop and listen.

Some Remedies and Workarounds

- ☐ **1. Anxious? Build up your confidence.** Take a course or work with a tutor to build your confidence in one area at a time. Focus on the strengths you do have; think of ways you can use them to your benefit. If you're an expert in an area, imagine yourself calmly delivering key maps.

- ☐ **2. Unsure where to start? Study leaders with strong presence.** Leading is greatly aided by presence. You have to look and sound like a leader. Study people who have a commanding presence. Pay attention to their voice modulation, change of pace, eye contact, gestures, and so on. Do you dress the part? Do you sound confident? Do you complain or do you project an image of someone who solves problems? Giving presentations and looking the part is a known technology. Go to a course; join Toastmasters. Get coaching from an acting director. Act a scene in a pretend play called *Presence*.

27

174

☐ **3. Unclear message? Focus on the essence.** When speaking to someone or a group, state your message or purpose in a single sentence, then outline your pitch around three to five things that support this thesis and that you want people to remember. Consider what someone should be able to say 15 minutes after you finish. Don't try to tell the audience all you know, even if they are well-informed on the topic. You are giving a persuasive argument or communicating key information; it's not a lecture. Drowning people in detail will lose even the knowledgeable and the interested. Practice out loud. Writing out a pitch or argument isn't useful until you say it. Writing sounds stilted when spoken because the cadence of speech and sentence length is generally quite different.

☐ **4. Wary of criticism? Prepare in advance.** Leading is risky. You have to defend what you're doing, so convince yourself first that you are on the right track. Be prepared to explain again and again, to attract lightning bolts from detractors, from those unsettled by change and from those who will always say it could have been done differently, better, and cheaper. To prepare for this, think about the 10 objections that will come up, and mentally rehearse how you will reply. Listen patiently to people's concerns, acknowledge them, then explain why you think the change will be beneficial. Attack positions, but not people.

☐ **5. Unaware/uncertain of your impact? Get critical feedback.** Be more real. Seek critical feedback. Others view people who seek critical feedback more positively. People who seek only positive feedback get the opposite response. The former shows willingness to improve. The latter is often seen as defensiveness and a disinterest in really knowing oneself. Disclose more. If you deny, minimize, or excuse away mistakes and shortcomings, take a chance and admit that you're imperfect like everyone else. Let your inside thoughts out in the open more often. Take personal responsibility. Admit mistakes matter-of-factly, inform everyone potentially affected, learn from it so the mistake isn't repeated, then move on. Successful people make lots of mistakes. All of this adds to a positive presence.

☐ **6. One-way communicator? Listen more.** Do you really know how others see the issue or do you just tell and sell? Do you even know if it is important to them? Don't interrupt. Don't suggest words or solutions when they pause. Don't cut them off by saying, "I already know that," "I've heard that before," or the dreaded "But I know that won't work." Be a two-way person. Practice reciprocity. Try to follow the rule of exchange. They get something, you get something. Build your presence by being more open, sharing, and giving.

☐ **7. Lacking polish? Choose your words more carefully.** Eliminate poor speech habits such as using the same words repeatedly, using filler words like "uh" and "you know," speaking too rapidly or forcefully, or going into so much detail that people can't follow the map. Avoid condescending terms like "What you need to understand" or "This is the third time...." Both imply the receiver is either stupid or unwilling. Don't use words that are personal, blaming, or autocratic. Outline arguments. Know the three things you're trying to say and say them succinctly. Others can always ask questions if something is unclear.

☐ **8. Lacking good mentors or models for presence? Study what great actors do.** Using acting as a model for building presence, there are several aspects of the stage performance that enter into the actor's skills:

– The first is the significance of the entrance. People tend to form short-term impressions based on little other than the manner of entrance, the physical characteristics of the actor, and the words and non-verbal behaviors in the first few moments. Think about the impression you want to leave. Vision your entrance. Does it leave the message you intend. Do you look, act, and sound your intended presence?

– Next is establishing your voice. Voice has three elements. The first is the actual delivery voice. Volume. Tone. Speed. Language. Articulation. The second is non-verbals. Do your non-verbals (gestures, posture, facial expressions, movement) align with your message? The next is content. Are you confident and knowledgeable? Is it apparent that you know what you are talking about? Do you know your lines?

– The next element of presence is audience engagement. How do you intend to engage the audience? Is this going to be participative? Does the audience have a role? Do they know what it is you expect? Are you in command of your audience?

– The last element of presence is the exit. How do you intend to wrap things up? Do you have a strong close? Have you planned how you are going to end and finish by leaving your audience with the thoughts and conclusions you intended?

For the actor, these are the elements of creating a strong stage presence. It's not that different in the world of work. Everything matters. Taken all together, they build presence.

☐ **9. Lacking boldness? Tap into your passion.** If you're tired of what you're doing, find something for which you have enthusiasm. Appoint yourself as champion of the change. Throw out trial balloons to see if your notion spurs some interest. Find an experimenter to go in with you. Bring in a heavy expert. Plant seeds at every opportunity.

☐ **10. (Workaround) Not motivated to build presence? Market other aspects of yourself.** If you are not blessed with presence and do not want to work

27

to increase it, learn to market other aspects of yourself. Set up a marketing plan. What are you good at? What have you accomplished? What would others be interested to know about you? How can you help them be more successful? In order to make up for a lack of presence, you need substance and content. Through those aspects of yourself, you can get respect and probably get a following of people interested in working with and for you.

More Help?

In addition to the 10 tips listed for this dimension, there are some tips that may apply from *FYI For Your Improvement*™. We have coded each item to about 10 tips from the *FYI* book. To use this resource, the codes below refer to the chapter and then the tip number from the *FYI* book. For example, in item 27 below, 1-1,4 refers to Chapter 1 – Action Oriented, tips 1 and 4. If you don't have a copy of *FYI*, it is available through Lominger International at 952-345-3610 or www.lominger.com.

27. People feel more confident when this person is in charge.

　　1-1,4; 9-1,3,4,5,8,10; 53-1; 60-1

54. Exudes self-confidence.

　　1-4; 9-1,2,3,4,5,8,10; 107-1; 108-2

81. Has a significant, noticeable presence.

　　1-4; 8-1; 9-1,2,3,5,10; 34-7; 107-1; 108-2

Jobs That Would Add Skills in This Dimension

☐ Chair of Projects/Task Forces – requiring finding new and effective solutions under tight deadlines and high visibility on an issue that matters to people higher up.

☐ Crisis Manager or Change Manager – requiring quick, tough-minded decisions under tight time pressure with a low level of consultation and more resting on one person's thinking and actions than is typical.

☐ Fix-Its/Turnarounds – requiring making tough decisions impacting a variety of people and constituencies on a tight schedule with little room for error and the weight of the thinking and plan resting on one person.

☐ Scale (size shift) Assignments – impacting larger numbers of people with many of them remote and dispersed.

☐ Significant People Demands – requiring managing a large number of people, usually in dispersed structures.

☐ Start-Ups – requiring forging a new team and initiating a number of simultaneous actions with little guidance from the past under a tight time frame with the major burden of thinking and actions on one person.

27

Part-Time Assignments That Would Add Skills in This Dimension

☐ Manage a group of people involved in tackling a fix-it or turnaround project.

☐ Relaunch an existing product or service that's not doing well.

☐ Manage a group of balky and resisting people through an unpopular change or project.

☐ Manage a group through a significant business crisis.

☐ Take on a tough and undoable project, one where others who have tried it have failed.

☐ Assemble a team of diverse people to accomplish a difficult task, or build a multi-functional project team to tackle a common business issue or problem.

☐ Manage a group including former peers to accomplish a task.

☐ Integrate diverse systems, processes, or procedures across decentralized and/or dispersed units.

☐ Manage a group of people who are older and/or more experienced to accomplish a task.

☐ Prepare and present a proposal of some consequence to top management.

☐ Be a change agent; create a symbol for change; lead the rallying cry; champion a significant change and implementation.

☐ Manage a group of "green," inexperienced people as their coach, teacher, guide, etc.

☐ Manage a temporary group of low-competence people through a task they couldn't do by themselves.

☐ Handle a tough negotiation with an internal or external client or customer.

Confidence is contagious. So is lack of confidence.
Vince Lombardi – American football coach

27

Suggested Readings

Barnes, B. K. (2006). *Exercising influence workbook: A self-study guide.* San Francisco, CA: Pfeiffer.

Cohen, A. R., & Bradford, D. L. (2005). *Influence without authority* (2nd ed.). Hoboken, NJ: John Wiley & Sons.

Dowis, R. (2000). *The lost art of the great speech: How to write one – How to deliver it.* New York, NY: AMACOM.

Griffin, J. (2008). *How to say it at work: Power words, phrases, and communication secrets for getting ahead* (2nd ed.). Paramus, NJ: Prentice Hall.

Hernez-Broome, G., McLaughlin, C., & Trovas, S. (2007). *Selling yourself without selling out: A leader's guide to ethical self-promotion.* Greensboro, NC: Center for Creative Leadership.

Kheel, T. W. (2001). *The keys to conflict resolution: Proven methods of resolving disputes voluntarily.* New York, NY: Four Walls Eight Windows.

Koegel, T. J. (2007). *The exceptional presenter: A proven formula to open up and own the room.* Austin, TX: Greenleaf Book Group Press.

Kotter, J. P. (2008). *Power and influence: Beyond formal authority.* New York, NY: Free Press.

Manz, C. C., & Sims, H. P. (2001). *The new superleadership: Leading others to lead themselves.* San Francisco, CA: Berrett-Koehler Publishers.

McNally, D., & Speak, K. D. (2003). *Be your own brand: A breakthrough formula for standing out from the crowd.* San Francisco, CA: Berrett-Koehler Publishers.

Presentations Magazine. www.presentations.com.

Rein, I., Kotler, P., Hamlin, M., & Stoller, M. (2005). *High visibility: Transforming your personal and professional brand* (3rd ed.). New York, NY: McGraw-Hill.

Schiraldi, G. R. (2007). *10 Simple solutions for building self-esteem: How to end self-doubt, gain confidence and create a positive self-image.* Oakland, CA: New Harbinger Publications.

Ursiny, T. (2005). *The confidence plan: How to build a stronger you.* Naperville, IL: Sourcebooks, Inc.

27

27

Appendix A
Creating a Development Plan

Universal Ideas for Developing Any Skill

☐ **1. Choose wisely.** Figure out what is critically important to performance in your job or success in your career. This is a huge investment of your time and energy, so make sure that you're focused on something that matters to you and something that other people think is important, too. Be realistic about what you can accomplish. Refer to the Developmental Difficulty level to see how difficult it is to develop the learning agility Dimension(s) you've selected. Make sure they don't all fall in the "harder to develop" category. Keep that in mind when you create your action plan and set your time frame. You will feel more motivated and be more committed to your development when you feel successful and see improvement.

☐ **2. Get specific.** Get more detailed and behavioral feedback on the need. Most of the time, people are weak in some aspect of a skill. To find out more about what your need is specifically, go to a few people who know and who will tell you if you ask. Accept that you have a need. Don't be defensive or try to rationalize away the need. Say you are concerned about the need and request more detailed information so you can focus on an efficient plan for growth and development. Ask them for specific examples. When? Where? With whom? In what settings? Under what conditions? How many times? Might anyone they know be of help? Get as specific as you can. Listen, don't rebut. Take notes. Thank them for the input.

☐ **3. Create the plan.** If you have accepted the need as true and you are ready to do something about it, you need three kinds of action plans. You need to know what to stop doing, start doing, and keep doing. Since you have a need in this area (you don't do this well), you need to stop some things you are doing that aren't working. In their place, you need to start doing some things you either don't like doing, haven't ever done, or don't even know about. Even if you are bad at something, there are things you do in this area that you are probably good at. Send a form or e-mail to a number of people who would be willing to help you work on this skill. Tell them you have discovered and taken ownership of this need, want to do something about it, list the specific need you discovered in step one, and ask them for the things you should stop doing, start doing, and keep doing.

☐ **4. Learn from others.** Research shows that we learn best from others when we (a) Pick multiple models, each of whom excels at one thing rather than looking for the whole package in one person. Think more broadly than your current job for models; add some off-work models. (b) Take both the student and the teacher role. As a student, study other people—don't just admire or dislike what they do. Reduce what they do or don't do to a set of principles or rules of thumb to integrate into your behavior. As a teacher, it's one of the best ways to learn something as it forces you to think it through and be concise in your explanation. (c) Rely on multiple methods of learning—interview people, observe them without speaking with them, study remote models by reading books or watching films, get someone to tutor you, or use a contrast strategy. Sometimes it's hard to see the effects of your behavior because you are too close to the problem. Pick two people, one who is much better than you are at your need and one who is much worse. Copy what the good model does that leads to good outcomes. Get rid of the behaviors that match what the bad model does. Or, get a partner. If you can find someone working on the same need, you can share learnings and support each other. Take turns teaching each other some to do's, one of the best ways to cement your learning. Share books you've found. Courses you've attended. Models you've observed. You can give each other progress feedback.

☐ **5. Read the "bible" on this need.** Every skill or competency has had one or more books written about it: How to negotiate to win. How to get along with bad bosses. How to win friends. How to be more creative. Go to a large business bookstore and buy at least two books covering your need. Take one hour and scan each book. Just read the first sentence of every paragraph. Don't read to learn. Just read to see the structure of the book. Pick the one that seems to be right for you and read it thoroughly. That book may reference or lead you to other books or articles on the skill. Use your reading to answer the following questions: What's the research on the skill? What are the 10 how-to's all the experts would agree to? How is this skill best learned?

☐ **6. Learn from autobiographies and biographies.** Find books by or on two famous people who have the skill you are trying to build. Try to see how they wove the skill you are working on into their fabric of skills. Was there a point in their lives when they weren't good at this skill? What was the turning point?

☐ **7. Learn from a course.** Find the best course you have access to. It might be offered in your organization or, more likely, it will be a public program. Find one that is taught by the author of a book or a series of articles on this need. Be sure to give it enough time. It usually takes three to five days to learn about any skill or competency. One- to two-day courses are usually not long enough. Find one where you learn the theory and have a lot of practice with the skill. Find one that videotapes if the skill lends itself to the lens. Take your detailed plan with you and take notes against your need. Don't just take notes following the course outline. For example, if you're attending a listening course and one of your need statements is how to listen when people ramble, take notes against that specific statement; or if your need involves a task or project, write down action steps you can take immediately. Throw yourself into the course. No phone calls. Don't take any work with you. No sightseeing. Just do the course. Be the best student in the course and learn the most. Seldom will a course alone be sufficient to address a need. A course always has to be combined with the other remedies in this Universal Development Plan, especially stretching tasks, so you can perform against your need under pressure.

☐ **8. Try some stretching tasks, but start small.** Seventy percent of skills development happens on the job. As you talk with others while building this skill, get them to brainstorm tasks and activities you can try. Write down five tasks you will commit to doing, tasks like: initiate three conversations, make peace with someone you've had problems with, write a business plan for your unit, negotiate a purchase, make a speech, find something to fix. You can try tasks off the job as well: teach someone to read, be a volunteer, join a study group, take up a new hobby—whatever will help you practice your need in a fairly low-risk way. After each task, write down the positive and negative aspects of your performance and note things you will try to do better or differently next time.

☐ **9. Track your own progress.** You are going to need some extra motivation to get through this. You need to be able to reward yourself for progress you've made. Others may not notice the subtle changes for a while. Set progress goals and benchmarks for yourself. Keep a log. Make a chart. Celebrate incremental progress.

☐ **10. Get periodic feedback.** Get a group of people who haven't known you for long. They don't have a history of seeing you not do well in this skill over a long period of time. Get feedback from them a third of the way into your skill-building plan. Also, go back to the original group who helped you see and accept this need. Their ratings will lag behind the first group because they know your history in this skill. Use both groups to monitor your progress.

A

Development Plan

The following pages provide you with a Development Plan template where you can record your development need and action plan.

PERMISSION TO COPY DEVELOPMENT PLAN: *This confirms that Lominger International: A Korn/Ferry Company is granting you the right to make copies of My Development Need on pages A-6 through A-9 of* FYI *for Learning Agility™ appendix. Such copies are for the internal use of your organization only. All copies must retain the copyright notice located on the bottom of each page.*

(Sample) My Development Need:

Dimension 14: Open Minded
Factor II: People Agility

LEARNER NAME:
TO BE COMPLETED BY:

MY "BEFORE" DESCRIPTION (Unskilled)	SOME CAUSES FOR ME
Not particularly open to different viewpoints. *Prefer tried-and-true solutions.*	*Perfectionist.* *Not observant.*

MY LEARNINGS FROM "THE MAP"

I don't always seek more viewpoints or look at issues as a means to learn something.

A-6

QUOTES THAT INSPIRE ME

"The open-minded see the truth in different things: the narrow-minded see only the differences." – Author Unknown

MY ACTION PLAN
(Development Remedies, Workarounds, Jobs, Part-Time Assignments)

14.2 – Work on understanding without judging. Ask more questions, be a detective.

14.6 – Generate multiple solutions, don't settle on the first one.

Workaround:
14.10 – Check my viewpoints with a disinterested person first before I disclose them.

Job:
Cross-Move – requiring working with a new group of people.

Part-Time Assignment:
Assemble a team of diverse people to accomplish a difficult task.

MY "AFTER" DESCRIPTION
(Skilled)

Open to new ideas, solutions.

Can change my mind.

MY SUGGESTED READINGS

Active Listening: Improve Your Ability to Listen and Lead (2006) by M. H. Hoope.

A-7

My Development Need:

....
....
....

LEARNER NAME: ....
TO BE COMPLETED BY: ....

MY "BEFORE" DESCRIPTION (Unskilled)	SOME CAUSES FOR ME

MY LEARNINGS FROM "THE MAP"

QUOTES THAT INSPIRE ME

MY ACTION PLAN
(Development Remedies, Workarounds, Jobs, Part–Time Assignments)

MY "AFTER" DESCRIPTION
(Skilled)

A

MY SUGGESTED READINGS

A

Appendix B
Competency Summary

Top 22 Leadership Architect® Competencies Most Associated with Choices Architect® 2nd Edition Items

1. *Dealing with* Ambiguity (2)
2. Problem Solving (51)
3. Learning on the Fly (32)
4. Perspective (46)
5. Conflict Management (12)
6. Sizing Up People (56)
7. Listening (33)
8. *Dealing with* Paradox (40)
9. Standing Alone (57)
10. Personal Learning (45)
11. Patience (41)
12. Process Management (52)
13. Creativity (14)
14. Understanding Others (64)
15. Composure (11)
16. Motivating Others (36)
17. Organizing (39)
18. Self-Knowledge (55)
19. Command Skills (9)
20. Political Savvy (48)
21. *Managing* Diversity (21)
22. *Timely* Decision Making (16)

B

B